MW01148844

Can It!
START CANNING AND PRESERVING TODAY

BY JACKIE CALLAHAN PARENTE

HOBBY
H/F
FARM
PRESS

Can It!

Project Team
Lead Editor: Jennifer Calvert
Senior Editor: Amy Deputato
Associate Editor: Lindsay Hanks
Art Director: Jerome Callens
Book Project Specialist: Karen Julian
Production Supervisor: Jessica Jaensch
Assistant Production Manager: Tracy Vogtman
Indexer: Melody Englund

I-5 PUBLISHING, LLC™
Chief Executive Officer: Mark Harris
Chief Financial Officer: Nicole Fabian
Vice President, Chief Content Officer: June Kikuchi
General Manager, I-5 Press: Christopher Reggio
Editorial Director, I-5 Press: Andrew DePrisco
Art Director, I-5 Press: Mary Ann Kahn
Digital General Manager: Melissa Kauffman
Production Director: Laurie Panaggio
Production Manager: Jessica Jaensch
Marketing Director: Lisa MacDonald

Text Copyright © 2011 by I-5 Publishing, LLC™

Quote on page 4 Copyright © 1997 Garrison Keillor. Reprinted by permission of Garrison Keillor

Recipes for Kosher Dill Pickles on page 169 and Fiesta Salsa on page 175 provided by Jarden Home Brands, marketers of Ball® and Kerr® fresh preserving products. Jarden Home Brands is a division of Jarden Corporation (NYSE: JAH).

Front Cover Photography: Gina Cioli and Veronique Bos
Back Cover Photography: psrobin/Flickr

All rights reserved. No part of this book may be reproduced, stored in a retrieval system, or transmitted in any form or by any means, electronic, mechanical, photocopying, recording, or otherwise, without the prior written permission of I-5 Press™, except for the inclusion of brief quotations in an acknowledged review.

Library of Congress Cataloging-in-Publication Data
Parente, Jackie Callahan, 1947-
 Can it! : start canning and preserving today / Jackie Callahan Parente.
    p. cm.
 Includes bibliographical references and index.
 ISBN 978-1-935484-28-8 (pbk.)
 1. Canning and preserving. I. Title.
 TX603.P117 2012
 641.4'2--dc23
          2011028063

I-5 Publishing, LLC™
3 Burroughs, Irvine, CA 92618
www.facebook.com/i5press
www.i5publishing.com

Printed and bound in China
13 14 15 16 17   3 5 7 9 8 6 4 2

Dedication

To Dad, who taught me how to save, and to Mom, who taught me how to preserve.

Acknowledgments

Many people and many organizations offered their generous assistance in writing this book. It's impossible to envision writing it without paying homage to the icons that have made home food preservation accessible, enjoyable, and safe. The folks at Ball Corporation and the United States Department of Agriculture (USDA) have instructed generations of canners in the safe preparation of delicious home-preserved foods. Dog-eared copies of their guides are fixtures in my kitchen library; copies of their most recent editions with all current safe-processing guidelines served as a constant reference when writing this volume.

I would like to especially acknowledge Stephanie Shih from Jarden Home Brands, the folks who market Ball and Kerr fresh-preserving supplies. Jarden Home Brands generously granted me permission to use any of their delicious recipes. Many of the ones in this volume are recipes that have been in my kitchen for years (but most likely have their origins in my first Ball recipe book!). When necessary for validation and to ensure food safely, I relied on the authority of the Ball guides and the USDA instructions.

The staffs at various Cooperative Extension Services, especially at the University of Connecticut, were—as always—helpful, supportive, and informative in all things related to food safety and gardening. (I encourage you to use this valuable resource in your community!)

Garrison Keillor and his staff at Prairie Home Productions, LLC generously granted rights to the opening quote from *Mother Father Uncle Aunt*, a quote that was both inspirational in my writing and reminiscent to me of times past. Special thanks also go to Steve Lehman, Acquisitions Manager at HighBridge Audio, who helped me navigate the permissions maze and graciously tolerated my incessant badgering.

This book would not have been possible without the vision of the folks at I-5 Press. Andrew DePrisco and Karen Julian helped me develop the concept and encouraged me throughout the writing. With a balanced and friendly combination of coaching and cajoling, editor Jennifer Calvert helped me to transform a somewhat unwieldy manuscript into a book that's accessible, useful, and fun.

Loving appreciation and admiration goes to my sister, Suzy Bosl, who has been my mentor in canning and freezing for years. She scoured the recipe books of family and friends to unearth many of the gems shared here.

And lastly, gratitude beyond measure to my children and husband, Bob, who have encouraged me both during the writing of this book and throughout my professional and preserving careers. I'll repay you in the only way I know: red raspberry jam, sweet relish, and canned applesauce.

"When I was a boy, the way that you combated the winter blues was very simple. You went down the basement. You went to the shelves that were behind the washtub and reached up there and there were all your mother's canned vegetables, and jams, and peaches, and there was corn, there was applesauce, and apple butter. And you reached down to the end and you got a jar of stewed tomatoes. You took that up and you took off the lid and you put some of it in a pan, and you heated it up, and you put butter on it. And in those stewed tomatoes that you yourself picked and helped your mother can last August, you found in those tomatoes the courage or sunshine or whatever it was that you needed to buck yourself up and get on with winter and not complain about it, and of course, those were Ball canning jars!"

—Garrison Keillor, *Mother Father Uncle Aunt*

Contents

Introduction

The Garrison Keillor quote on the previous page comes from a March 15, 1997, performance of *A Prairie Home Companion* performed in Muncie, Indiana. Keillor was playing to his audience with his monologue titled, "Ball Jars." Muncie is home to the canning icon, Ball Corporation. As he is known to do in his monologues, Keillor waxes both philosophical and sentimental on the topic of food preservation. He playfully makes the statement that, in his (mythical) childhood home of Lake Wobegon, "Home canning was the basis of a whole social order."

As humorous as his monologue is, there is truth in Keillor's words. Home food preservation has been a fundamental human activity until more recent generations, when developed societies migrated to industrialized farming and food preparation. Food preservation is as old as civilization. People have always endeavored to devise safe means to extend the useful life of the food that they have found, grown, caught, or killed. During the nineteenth and early twentieth century, many families enjoyed the benefits of home-grown/raised produce and meat, and they preserved them using a variety of familiar methods including canning, drying, salting, smoking, and, later, freezing. The second half of the twentieth century saw the emergence of mega-grocery stores, food warehouses, convenience foods, fast foods, industrial farming, and the wane of home food preservation. Our busy, dual-income, multitasking families embraced convenience and fast foods, while putting Grandma's canner on a dusty shelf or, more likely, in a tag sale. Times change and so does a society's perspective. As the twenty-first century enters its second decade, economic issues, concern for food safety and nutrition, and a heightened awareness for global environmental concerns are foremost. Many people are revisiting home food preservation for a variety of reasons—some that are consistent with earlier generations, such as economy and wholesome food, and others that are unique to contemporary needs.

But this renaissance poses a number of questions in the minds of the new would-be preservationist. *Mom and Grandma aren't around to show me how to do this. How can I be sure that I'm doing it right? Is it hard? Could I poison my family? What's the best method: canning, freezing, or drying? Can city-dwellers get into home food preservation?* The stream of questions is almost endless, and the good news/bad news is that the stream of answers is, too. How does the neophyte get started without a PhD-level investment in learning?

Breathe easy. As a *Wall Street Journal* headline once stated, "Yes, You Can." Home food preservation is not only possible for the uninitiated, but it's also *fun*! This book is intended to bring together old-school basics and today's need for accurate, easily accessible, and succinct instructions. I've designed it so that you can quickly get *just* the information that you need.

Are you new to home food preservation? Concerned about safety, nutrition, and sustainability? Focus on chapters 1 and 2. You'll gain an historical perspective, while reviewing the many benefits of home preservation and learning about food safety and spoilage issues. You'll see that today's home food-preservation techniques go far beyond the Mason jar. Chapter 2 helps you choose home food-preservation methods that best support your objectives in terms of nutrition, ease, and sustainability. Many folks have strong opinions about what method is best. Bottom line: what is best is whatever works for you and your family.

Equipped with information about the scope of food procurement and preservation, you can choose the chapter that gives you specifics about the method you're most interested in. Look at chapters 3 through 6 for details on each of the various preservation methods that we cover: freezing, canning (water bath and pressure), making jellies and jams, and pickling and fermenting. This book offers a concise survey of safe preservation methods along with tasty and convenient recipes. Because sustainability is in the forefront of many people's minds, I offer tips and options that are eco-friendly.

You will also find handy reference information in the appendix, such as conversion charts, techniques, and more. This book is a great first step into the world of home food preservation, and when you're ready to take bigger steps, you can check out the list of resources I've compiled for you at the back of the book.

Enjoy the adventure of home food preservation! It's a hobby that easily turns into a lifestyle.

CHAPTER 1

A Contemporary Perspective

Food preservation has been a part of our human discourse since the dawn of civilization. From the perspective of the twenty-first century, the needs and motives of our ancestors may feel remote. But it is no less true now than it was millennia ago: you are what you eat. What *has* changed is the society in which we live and the food growing, gathering, processing, and preservation options now available to us. We learned that we could maximize the crop yields through monoculture, chemical fertilizers and pesticides, and industrial-size farming implements. We stopped taking ownership of our food gathering and learned to rely on commercial resources, often under the questionable banner of "convenience." Dual-income families with an average of two-and-one-third children who played soccer, tennis, piano, and more didn't have the time to cook a meal let alone consider the possibility of home food preservation. Today, much of our food "grows" in the cans, bottles, and cello packs that line our grocery shelves. Or even more conveniently, our meals come to us fully prepared through an anonymously staffed drive-through window. Unlike our ancestors, we have many and varied choices regarding how we gather and store our food. Food gathering doesn't need to be delegated to nameless industrial farms and processing plants. If we want, we can take ownership of some or all of this food stewardship. While the degree of urgency may feel different today than it did for other civilizations throughout history, the core values are the same: preserve good, healthy food when it's abundant to sustain us during times of scarcity.

If you picked up this volume, you are most likely choosing to take a more hands-on approach than many in our society. Let's explore some of the reasons why taking this ownership of home food preservation makes sense today—how it can be convenient, safe, satisfying, and nutritious. We'll take a short look back at some of the history, and we'll look at some more contemporary issues of sustainability.

THE REAL CONVENIENCE FOOD

What's more convenient than going out to the garden and picking tomatoes for your salad? Perhaps stepping into your pantry for a jar of canned tomatoes.

My mother grew up in poverty on a farm in Ohio. When she was a child, her family had no choice but to maximize what they took out of the soil and use or preserve every scrap. As her child a generation later, I helped her can and freeze the fruits and vegetables that we grew. We'd freeze sides of beef and pork that we had ordered from local farmers. With this stored bounty, we could spend the winter tapping into the jars on the shelves under the basement stairs and the goods frozen in our large chest freezer. Having grown up in the 1950s, I also remember how so-called convenience foods began to appear in our kitchen and on our supper table. Processed foods with extended shelf lives seemed to make food storage and preparation easier. As we all know, that trend became the norm.

Without getting into the fray of arguments between industrialized food and sustainable farming, let's revisit this notion of convenience food and dispel some of the fallacies surrounding home food preservation:

♣ Are convenience foods really more convenient than home-preserved foods?

♣ Are preserved foods always less nutritious than fresh ones?

♣ Is home food preservation really feasible for today's hyper-busy population?

Convenience is subjective, of course. But with a little planning and about the time you would spend watching one episode of your favorite sitcom, you can have a number of wholesome meals sitting in the freezer. And having a winter's worth of vegetables, fruits, and meats stored under your own roof can save you some visits to the grocery store. That seems pretty convenient. Want to give some very special holiday gifts without enduring the hassle and expense of shopping? Who wouldn't be thrilled to get a jar of your homemade jam, pickles, or salsa? It's easy to create custom labels and pretty packaging, too.

"But home food preservation is too complicated," you protest. "Myth," I retort. First, you do not need to have an advanced degree or special training to put away food that is safe and nutritious. Current generations do lack the personal tutoring that was available for prior generations, but you'll find plenty of support available through your local Cooperative Extension Service, the United States Department of Agriculture (USDA), and canning and preserving groups such as Canning Across America, which orchestrated a nationwide "canvolution" and National Can-

Home-preserving isn't only about "putting up" jars of grape jelly and dill pickles. Recipes abound that will tempt your taste buds in unexpected ways.

It-Forward Day to raise awareness of and support interest in canning. And according to Jarden Home Brands (makers of Ball- and Kerr-brand Mason jars, based in Daleville, Indiana), industry sales of canning equipment were up 35 percent in 2011. That means there are a lot of folks who are interested in getting back to home food preservation, so you're sure to find a buddy.

IT'S ONLY NATURAL

My son stopped by for supper last night. He's definitely a foodie, with a strong interest in organic gardening, but he also lives on a shoestring, with a strong interest in economical foods. For dessert, we had a compote of frozen, locally grown peaches; my homemade chocolate raspberry sauce; and homemade vanilla yogurt. "It's cheaper to make your yogurt than it is to buy it, right, Mom?" he asked. I really wanted to give him the answer he was looking for and respond emphatically, "Yes, of course it is." The answer is, "It depends." We won't go into the cost-benefit numbers here because they are dependent upon a range a variables. From my personal experience, some foods, such as jams and pickles, are cheaper when you preserve them yourself. For most other fruits and vegetables that I preserve, it's hard to compete with commercial canneries and warehouse food prices. But I don't "put up" (canning lingo for "preserve") my food for the economics of it. I do it for the joy of being my own food steward.

If you grow your own produce or can walk up and shake the hand of the guy who did, you're more likely to know exactly what you're getting in that jar of applesauce.

When you preserve your own food, you enjoy the benefit of knowing exactly where your food came from, how old it is, and what's in the container along with your food. Consider a recent newspaper headline, "BPA Found in Almost All Canned Food." When you do your own food preservation, stories about bisphenol-A and other harmful by-products aren't troublesome.

For those who are concerned about chemical additives and preservatives, sodium and sugar levels, and large amounts of high-fructose corn syrup, to name just a few of the current food-related issues, there is comfort in controlling these factors. When you preserve your own food, there's no need to read ingredient labels so conscientiously. There are no mysterious ingredients hiding behind a hand-penned label that reads "Tomatoes, July 2012." That's just good, wholesome food!

THE SOONER, THE BETTER

Home food preservation isn't difficult, but it does require some forethought. Fruits and vegetables are at their peak in terms of flavor and nutrition at the moment they are picked. This is as good as it gets— canning or freezing will not improve the quality. Every minute that separates the time of picking from the moment of preservation causes a loss of quality and nutrition in the product. Thus, it's very important to plan your picking or visit to the farmer's market so that you can preserve the bounty quickly. My mother told me not to bother making pickles if the cukes were even a day old! Some vegetables are more time sensitive than others, but all experts agree that soonest is best.

BUT IS IT NUTRITIOUS?

Those who claim that the preserved version cannot compete with its fresh counterpart and that frozen is far better than canned alternatives haven't read the fine print when it comes to nutritional values. Eating fresh-picked fruits or vegetables is best, but if you want something "fresh" in February in New England, going to your local grocery—even the high-end, overpriced boutiques—won't ensure that you will get fresh vegetables and fruits with the highest nutritional value. If your produce has been trucked or flown in from distant parts of the country or world, in addition to upping the carbon footprint, they have left much of their nutrients in the cargo hold. Compare these "fresh" fruits and vegetables to those that you've canned, frozen, or dried just minutes after the harvest. While it's indisputable that freshly picked local produce offers the highest quality in terms of taste and nutrition, information from unbiased sources such as the University of California at Davis, the University of Illinois, and the US Food and Drug Administration (FDA), show that if you choose to freeze, can, or otherwise preserve your summer harvest, you will most likely enjoy nutritional benefits equal to or better than the produce at your grocery. And considering the cost of produce during the off-season, your summer investment should be both tasty and economical.

If you find yourself gobbling up canned peaches from the supermarket, why not try to can some at home? Find fresh peaches at a local orchard for the best flavor and nutrition.

A BIT OF HISTORY

Because food begins to spoil the moment is it harvested or killed, people throughout history have sought to develop safe ways to preserve the bounty of today for use tomorrow. Food preservation enabled ancient hunter/gatherers to settle in one place, put down roots—figuratively and literally—and begin to enjoy the benefits of civilization. People have employed various methods of preservation tailored to their circumstances and their needs, in much the same fashion as we do today. The primary methods were drying, freezing/cold storage, fermenting, pickling, curing, making jams and jellies using fruit and sugar or honey, and more recently, canning.

WHERE IT BEGAN

Evidence suggests that the oldest form of preservation was drying. Middle Eastern and Asian cultures as early as 12,000 BC dried their food in the hot sun. Dried foods allowed seafarers to extend the range of their explorations, eventually circumnavigating the globe. Fermentation was discovered accidentally when a few grains of barley were left in the rain. Through fermentation, microorganisms changed (fermented) starch-derived sugars into alcohols. This process had multiple benefits: food was more nutritious, more palatable, and in many cases, produced an alcoholic beverage—nectar of

Home food preservation is certainly nothing new. One of the first preservation methods was drying foods in the sun. Dried fruits certainly haven't lost favor over time.

the gods! Curing and pickling both employed substances to change the chemistry of the food being preserved. In the case of pickling, vinegar and other acidic materials were found to provide climates unfriendly to the bacteria responsible for food spoilage, thus extending a food's usable life. Curing utilized salt, nitrites, and smoke to preserve foods, inhibit the growth of *Clostridium botulinium* (botulism), and improve the taste and color of the food.

The same foods that could be preserved by being dried could also be successfully preserved using other methods, such as freezing. Cranberries are a good example of this.

Freezing and cold storage were initially limited by geography. The 1800s brought the discovery of mechanical refrigeration, and eventually Clarence Birdseye perfected quick-freezing. While cold storage would significantly slow down the biological processes that caused the food to spoil and decompose, freezing would stop them altogether.

WHERE CANNING COMES IN

While it seems like an honorable old convention, canning is really the newcomer on the home food-preservation scene. In the 1790s, French confectioner and father of canning Nicolas Appert experimented for nearly fifteen years in an attempt to win an award offered by French emperor Napoleon Bonaparte, who needed a practical way to feed his armies. Appert's efforts were successful: he discovered that applying heat to food in sealed glass bottles helped to prevent food deterioration. Not only did he win Bonaparte's award, but the House of Appert became the first commercial cannery in the world. While Appert's methods were widely applied—meat, vegetables, fruit, and milk were processed in glass bottles and, later, tin cans—it wasn't until Louis Pasteur that we really understood *why* the heat application helped preserve the food. Pasteur's discovery of pasteurization in 1864 clarified the relationship between microorganisms, food spoilage, and illness, which we'll discuss in the next chapter.

REALLY GREEN GREENS: A WORD ABOUT SUSTAINABILITY

It is hard to argue that a venerable institution such as home food preservation—including canning, freezing, perfecting homemade jams and jellies, and the like—could be anything *but* green and sustainable. A Carnegie Mellon University study reports that 11 percent of the average American's household food-related greenhouse gas emissions come from the transportation of foods. According to that study, in the United States, food travels an average of 4,000 to 5,000 miles from its source to our table. Certainly, if you are home-canning locally grown produce, you are reducing the environmental impact of transporting produce across the country and around the world in off-seasons.

Think about it: peaches that travel thousands of miles to get to your supermarket are certainly going to be less fresh, flavorful, and nutritious than the peach you just plucked from the tree.

What's a Locavore?

This new word aptly describes a rapidly growing "species" of human in today's food-conscious society. Locavores want food that is fresh, healthy, sustainable, and *local*. No long-distance transportation that compromises the food quality, adds to the cost, and comes with a big carbon footprint. Locavores seek and savor seasonal foods that grow near them.

Canning your food is a great way to take control of what's in the food that you eat, ensuring that it's great-tasting and nutritious. You will most likely save a good amount of money in your food budget because you'll have your own supply of nutritious "convenience" foods. But as you are thinking about where and how you will get the foods that you want to can, don't forget the locavore's mantra: *think local.* It's true that you can sometimes get great bargains at wholesale food clubs, but think twice before you buy. The food that large wholesale clubs offer is often produced on industrialized farms using conventional growing methods (think pesticides, herbicides, genetically engineered seeds). It's likely picked before it's ripe so that it can withstand a long transport and handling time, during which it will have lost a great deal of its nutrients and fresh taste; and if it's transported over long distances, which such produce often is, distributors will have used a great deal of our energy resources (gas and oil for transport and electricity for refrigeration) to get your bargain produce from farm to store.

There are sustainable alternatives! Obviously, you can grow your own fruits and veggies. If you don't have adequate garden space where you live, perhaps your community offers garden plots that you can use or rent for a nominal fee during the growing season. Want the fruits of the labor without the actual labor? Join a Community Supported Agriculture (CSA) group and share in the bounty of local farmers. Check out local farmers' markets or farm stands. When produce is in season, you can often get very good prices by speaking directly with the farmer—and, most importantly, you get exceptionally fresh produce!

If you live in an urban area and don't have the space (or, perhaps, the inclination) to grow your own veggies, many urban neighborhoods have bountiful farmers' markets you can visit.

Combine gardening with home preservation and you will be living green and saving green, according to knowledgeable (albeit differing) sources. W. Atlee Burpee & Company, the largest seed and garden supply company in the United States, reports that families who garden will see a twenty-five-to-one return on their investment. The National Gardening Association also has positive (though more modest) claims. They state that a $70 investment in a garden will net a $600 harvest.

Of course, you want to be thoughtful about the food that you put into your body and the bodies of those dear to you. While it seems like home food preservation would, by its very nature, be a green, sustainable venture, it's not always that simple. You need to look beyond the immediacy of your choice—beyond the heart-tugging, high-profile claims of those on the green bandwagon—and look at the entire system of food preservation that you employ. Throughout this book, I will invite you to be thoughtful in your choices and to look at both short-term and long-term implications.

What does it really cost to can, freeze, dry, and so on? Yes, we want to eat locally and maximize the benefits of each growing season, but it's wise to balance your passion for sustainability by looking at all of the numbers, not just the ones that make the headlines. The cost of running that freezer 24/7 for twelve months a year is significantly more than the cost to can a batch of tomatoes. And that's only the consumer's cost of energy. What about the environmental impact of manufacturing the freezer and transporting it from factory to home…or the cost of producing the electricity to run the freezer? The choices can get sticky. Throughout this book, we'll include tips and tricks for keeping your food preservation wholesome, nutritious, sustainable, and fun! Now that we've covered much of the background, let's get started!

CHAPTER 2

Planning for Success

Getting started in home food preservation is really easy, but it does require some forethought and organization. In this chapter, we'll look into what types of food are suitable for home food preservation, the best and most sustainable way to get them, and how to choose a preservation method that fits your needs, all topped off with a short word about food safety and tips to help you plan successfully.

WHAT CAN YOU PRESERVE?

The short and easy answer is "just about everything," from seasonal fruits and vegetables to meats and seafoods, breads, dairy products, and entire meals. Scan the fruits and vegetables listed in the appendix to get a hint of the possibilities. But keep in mind that some things preserve better than others, so while you *can* can them, you might not want to.

WHERE TO START

Where can you find fresh produce for preserving? Obvious canning candidates are surplus vegetables from the garden. I always grow more tomatoes than I can possibly eat—and we eat lots of tomatoes when they are in season. Those wonderful tomatoes that don't get consumed in the summer months can be found in Mason jars in my basement as plain tomatoes or pasta sauce. Many are dried and stored with a bit of olive oil. If I don't have time to can them, I've been known to simply wash them and store them whole in the freezer.

Of course, don't forget about your local orchards and fruit farms during the season. My part of the country has incredible orchards and berry farms. I don't grow my own apples (yet), but my family and I love to go picking and return with a bushel of the apple *du jour*. You have myriad options for that bushel of apples (including many of the methods of food preservation that we'll cover in later chapters): canned applesauce; canned apple rings and apple pie filling; apple chutney; apple butter; and baked apple pies tucked away in the freezer for unexpected company. You can even turn those apples into a simple, wholesome baby food (see "Ava's Applesauce" on page 88).

Choose foods that your family enjoys most and then select a preservation method that suits your needs and the food's qualities. I adore my apples, but maybe you prefer peaches? The great thing about preserving food is that you have your own personal favorites on hand whenever you want them.

Create memories that you can cherish by picking fruit at a local orchard with your family and then preserving it together—in jellies and butters, for pies, and so on.

WHAT WORKS AND WHAT DOESN'T

If you're going to get into preserving, you'll need to learn which vegetables and fruits respond better to which preservation styles. For example, blueberries freeze very well and make delicious jams, syrups, or pies. At the other end of the berry spectrum are those fragile, voluptuous red raspberries. They are decadent when freshly picked and make exceptional jams, sauces, and flavored vinegar, but they turn to red mush when frozen. As you explore the different preservation methods and recipes in the chapters that follow, you'll learn what works and what doesn't. If you're a novice, start simple and build your technical skills.

Meats, seafood, and meat/vegetable-based sauces are all candidates for home preservation using various methods. The quickest, easiest, and safest one is freezing, but canning can offer a flexible and convenient alternative. If your family enjoys meats, contact a local farm and get a fresh side or quarter of beef (preferably grass fed), pork, or some free-range chickens. While you can preserve meat that you get from your local butcher or grocer, buying a local side of beef is generally less expensive and the meat is fresher.

Don't have a garden of your own to harvest? Look for local farms where you can pay a small price and pick as much fruit or as many veggies as you need for your home preservation project.

CHOOSING THE METHOD THAT'S RIGHT FOR YOU

You know your goal: to preserve food in season to enjoy out of season. That's simple. But within that overarching goal—and sometimes tangled in a sticky mess—are a number of other factors. Issues such as availability of a freezer or other storage space, dietary and/or nutritional preferences, and amount of time available—to name a few—have an impact on your choice of preservation method.

CONSIDER THE SOURCE

You can find lots of good information about food preservation and interesting recipes on the Web, but do be careful. Anyone can post anything to a website, but that doesn't ensure accuracy or safety. For example, I found an online jam recipe that called for sealing jam by turning over the newly filled jars for five minutes to kill the bacteria on the lid. This is an old-style method that's not approved by the US Department of Agriculture—the folks who help ensure food safety. Every method and recipe you'll read about in this book is written with your safety in mind.

Another point to remember as you review the various methods and their pros and cons is that these methods are all different tools in your preservation toolkit. The fact that they each have benefits and drawbacks does not make one inherently better than another. Each method simply serves a different need. Think about the appliances in your kitchen. There are times when a toaster oven is just perfect and others when your conventional oven makes more sense. The toaster oven draws less electricity per hour, but that doesn't mean that it's always the better tool to use. The same is true with preservation methods. The more options you have at your disposal, the more flexibility you'll have in developing your methods of preservation. Following are the various preservation types I'll cover, their pros and cons, and the foods most suitable for each method.

FREEZING AND FLASH FREEZING

Storing food in the freezer at 0 degrees Fahrenheit prevents microorganisms from growing and slowing down enzyme activity. Flash freezing is used to initially freeze food by rapidly lowering the temperature to -10 degrees Fahrenheit. This helps ensure the highest-quality frozen product. Once flash frozen, food can be stored at 0 degrees Fahrenheit. Freezing and flash freezing are best used for a range of foods, including fruits, vegetables, meats, jellies and jams, breads, and whole meals.

❖ **Pros:** This is the simplest of the common preservation methods (ideal for the food-preservation novice). Flavor retention is greater because it involves minimal heat processing. And this method has high degrees of success and food safety; microorganisms that can cause food spoilage are killed or become inactive when they're frozen.

Who hasn't experienced frozen peas—whether with dinner or on a bruised knee? If they're one of your favorites, growing your own peas and freezing them may be more economical.

❖ **Cons:** The amount of food you can preserve is limited to the size of your freezer. Stand-alone freezers involve significant financial investment that may take several years to pay off. This method has the most expensive cost for storage (depending upon size, age, style, and your local cost of electricity, running a freezer can cost anywhere between $5.00 and $25.00 per month).

WATER-BATH CANNING

After preserving food in glass jars using two-piece metal lids, you submerge the jarred food in a boiling-water bath for a specified period of time to destroy any harmful microorganisms and inactivate enzymes. Subsequent cooling creates a vacuum seal, which prevents air and other microorganisms from entering and causing spoilage. This method works well for

Think of all the pies you can make with home-preserved cherries or other tasty fruits. Turning your harvest into pantry staples is simple with water-bath canning.

a range of fruits, tomatoes, and other high-acid foods. You will also use water-bath canning to preserve jams, jellies, and other fruit-based soft spreads using primarily fruit and fruit juices together with a high sugar content. The high concentration of sugar helps prevent the growth of microorganisms. Pickles must also be water-bath canned. Using salt, vinegar, and other naturally occurring substances, the pickling process raises the acid level of the pickled food, creating an environment that is unfriendly to harmful microorganisms. Pickling is suitable for a range of vegetables, including cucumbers, peppers, cabbage, and cauliflower, as well as green tomatoes.

❖ **Pros:** Water-bath canning requires a low initial investment for equipment, electricity consumption for processing is modest, and there is no cost for storage.

❖ **Cons:** This method can cause some flavor and texture loss compared to freezing. The pickling process can take more than a month, depending upon the recipe.

PRESSURE CANNING

In this method, you also preserve food in glass jars with two-piece lids. Pressure canning must be used for low-acid foods and involves using an appliance called a—what else?—"pressure canner" to achieve a temperature of 240 degrees Fahrenheit, which is substantially higher

than the 212 degrees that the water-bath method can achieve and is sufficient to kill both microorganisms and their spores, including botulism, to which low-acid foods are vulnerable. As with water-bath canning, subsequent cooling creates a vacuum seal, which prevents air and microorganisms from entering and causing spoilage. This is the only safe way to can low-acid foods such as vegetables, meats, and seafood because of their susceptibility to botulism.

Corn is one of many vegetables that should be pressure-canned. To can corn, you'll need to cut it off the cob (individual recipes will explain how to do this).

❖ **Pros:** Pressure canning can also be used for high-acid foods such as tomatoes to lower the processing time. The electricity consumption for processing is moderate and there's no cost for storage.

❖ **Cons:** The initial investment for a pressure canner is somewhat costly. In addition, foods experience some flavor and nutrition loss compared to freezing. Pressure canning takes longer and is slightly more complicated than water-bath canning and freezing.

FOOD PRESERVATION IS NO PLACE FOR NOSTALGIA

So Grandma gave you her stack of worn and loved recipes for her pickles, jams, and canned corn. Brings back fond memories, doesn't it? You can put those recipes in a lovely commemorative book, but don't use them in your kitchen. To ensure food safety, you must follow accepted recipes—those that have been approved by the United States Department of Agriculture (USDA). Further, you must follow the recipes *exactly*, without adjusting the ingredients, proportions, type of processing, or processing time. Use only *current* information from reliable sources, such as your local Cooperative Extension Service, USDA Guides to Home Canning and Preserving, and other references listed in the Resources section of this book. Any instructions or recipes dated prior to 1988 are suspect because methods have changed.

SPOILAGE: SIMPLE BIOLOGY AND CHEMISTRY

Safe home food preservation is simply a matter of obeying the rules of biology and chemistry. If left to nature, food will spoil, become inedible, and possibly transmit bacteria. This is caused by naturally occurring processes and organisms. Home food preservation involves identifying them and creating environments that stop or retard the processes and destroy the organisms so that the food remains safe to eat.

If you've looked into home food preservation, you've surely heard about food that has spoiled and had to be discarded—or worse, horror stories about food poisoning and botulism. The truth is that some preserved food does spoil; on very rare occasions, this causes serious consequences. That's why it's very important to understand the mechanics of food spoilage and to **always follow safe food-preservation practices**. There is no one more vested in the safety of your food than you are!

Thoroughly washing your produce is one of the most important steps to creating a delcious and healthy product.

HOW ACID AND HEAT WORK TOGETHER IN FOOD PRESERVATION

If you're around food preservation circles it won't take long before you hear folks talk about high-acid and low-acid foods. This is a fundamental concept in food preservation because it serves as an index for measuring whether a particular food will provide a friendly or unfriendly environment for the invasion of microorganisms that cause food spoilage. The portion of this discussion that deals with high-acid and low-acid foods applies to canned foods only, not to frozen foods.

Some recipes will call for blanching vegetables (boiling or steaming and then rapidly cooling them). One of the reasons for blanching is to kill off some harmful microorganisms.

Like all creatures, the microorganisms that cause food spoilage are looking for a happy place to live and multiply. Many of them like it warm but not too warm. That's why we refrigerate our food—to delay spoilage. Some are sensitive to the amount of acid in a food. Most need some oxygen to thrive, which is why we seal the jars that we process. But some, such as the dreaded bacterium that causes botulism, prefer no oxygen. This can make things a bit tricky.

Understanding how microorganisms respond to heat, moisture, acid, and air helps us understand which food preservation method will be best for us.

HOT STUFF

First, let's look at how different microorganisms are affected by heat. See the table "Processing and Storage Temperatures for Food Preservation" for an illustration. There are three things that can cause your food to spoil: enzymes, fungi (molds and yeasts), and bacteria.

❖ **Enzymes** promote the changes that are a necessary part of that plant or animal's life cycle. Eventually, however, these enzymes change the food's color, flavor, and texture and make it unappetizing.

❖ **Molds** are fungi that grow on foods and look like fuzz. Some molds are harmless, but many more are not. These harmful molds produce mycotoxins, which can cause illness, and they thrive in high-acid environments, meaning they may eat the acid in a food that would otherwise protect that food from spoilage by bacteria. Molds are easily destroyed when heated to temperatures between 140 and 190 degrees Fahrenheit.

❖ **Yeasts** are fungi that cause food to ferment. This fermentation—while good in certain circumstances, such as those used in making pickles, bread, and beer—will often make food unfit to eat. As with molds, yeasts are easily destroyed when heated to temperatures between 140 and 190 degrees Fahrenheit.

❖ **Bacteria** are very different and can be more difficult to destroy. Some bacteria, notably the dreaded *Clostridium botulinum*, which causes deadly botulism poisoning, require a low-acid environment to live but can withstand temperatures much higher than yeasts, molds, and enzymes. As we said earlier, some bacteria thrive in environments where there is no oxygen. So, sealing the jar on these guys would just make them happy. And, bacteria produce spores, which—if not killed during processing—become bacteria that produce deadly toxins. While some bacteria will die at the same temperature as yeasts and molds, those pesky spores are much more resilient and require significantly higher temperatures to succumb.

Processing and Storage Temperatures for Food Preservation

TEMPERATURE	FOOD'S RESPONSE TO TEMPERATURE	DESCRIPTION
240°F	• This temperature kills bacteria and spores found in all food. • This is the only safe temperature for processing low-acid food.	This is the temperature you need to reach when pressure-canning.
150–212°F	• These temperatures kill most molds, yeasts, and bacteria in high-acid food, but they don't kill bacterial spores. • Higher temperatures decrease the time needed to kill microorganisms.	Water-bath canning reaches 212°F, and the average simmer begins at 190°F.
40–140°F	Danger! Between 40 and 140°F, bacteria, yeasts, and molds grow rapidly in unpreserved food.	95°F is the highest safe storage temperature for canned foods. Around 50°F is the best storage temperature.
32°F	Bacteria, yeasts, and molds grow slowly at cold temperatures.	Water freezes.
-10–0°F	Microorganisms do not grow in freezing temperatures, but some survive.	This is the ideal temperature for freezer storage.
-10°F	This temperature creates a sharp freeze.	This is the ideal temperature for flash-freezing foods.

HOW ACID FITS IN

The next component in canning is the acid level, or pH. Foods that are high in acid (*acidic*) call for different (some might say easier) means of preservation than foods that are low in acid (*alkaline*). See the table "Acidity and Safe Food Preservation" for some specific fruits and vegetables, but as a rule of thumb, fruits (including tomatoes) are high in acid while vegetables and meats are low in acid. Acidity is measured on a scale of pH values from 1 to 14, with 1 being the most acidic and 14 being the most alkaline. The midpoint on that scale (7) is neutral, but for our purposes, the tipping point is a pH level of 4.6. Thus, if a food has a pH value of 4.7 or higher, it will require different processing than foods that are 4.6 or lower. **Note: Foods with a pH value of 4.7 or higher cannot be safely processed in a water-bath canner.**

Acidity and Safe Food Preservation

TYPE OF SPOILAGE AGENT	MAXIMUM pH LEVEL THAT AN ORGANISM WILL SUSTAIN	TYPE OF FOOD	METHOD OF CANNING
	1 (Strongly Acidic)		
Molds	2		
Yeasts	3	Lemons	
		Pickles	
		Apricots	High-Acid Foods: safe to process at 212°F in a water-bath canner
		Plums	
		Apples	
		Peaches	
		Sauerkraut	
		Pears	
	4	Tomatoes	
Bacteria	4.6		Highest pH level that is safe to water-bath
	5	Figs	
		Okra	
		Carrots	Low-Acid Foods: safe to process at 240°F in a pressure canner
		Beets	
		Green Beans	
		Spinach	
	6		
	7	Corn	
		Peas	
	14 (Strongly Alkaline)		

TAKE BABY STEPS

When you try a new recipe, start small. Even recipes from reliable sources may not work out as well as you'd hoped. Just as you've tried recipes from great cookbooks and find that you simply don't like the way a recipe tastes, or that it doesn't look like the picture, the same can be true for any of the recipes involving food preservation. First time around, make just *one* batch. You've heard this before, but it's worth repeating: if you are a novice, start simply. Try water-bath canning or freezing. Freezing green beans is a snap (pun intended) and the results are great! Canning tomatoes or peaches is easy. Making strawberry freezer jam is even easier, but cooked jam is a breeze, too. You'll find recipes for these in the following chapters. Yes, it's tempting to want to triple the recipe or try something exotic. But starting small and simple helps you to quickly find what works best for you, and then grow your new skills with confidence.

PUTTING THEM TOGETHER

Now let's bring together the two key factors of acidity and heat. Remember, the high versus low acid determination only impacts food preserved by canning. If you are freezing food, acidity is irrelevant.

❖ **Foods that are high in acid** (generally fruits—including tomatoes—and pickled stuff that has a large amount of vinegar or lemon juice) can be successfully and safely preserved when you use a process that heats the food to a level that will kill the yeasts or mold (for example, water-bath canning at 212 degrees Fahrenheit) or reduce the temperature to a level that inhibits the growth (as with cold storage). Bacteria won't survive in the acid environment.

❖ **Foods that are low in acid** (generally vegetables and meats) can be successfully and safely preserved only when you use a process that heats the food to a level (240 to 250 degrees Fahrenheit with a pressure canner) that kills yeasts, molds, bacteria, and bacterial spores or that reduces the temperature to a level that inhibits their growth (as with cold storage).

A FINAL NOTE ON FOOD SAFETY

If this is beginning to sound complicated, remember one fundamental truth: if you follow accepted, tested methods and recipes, all of the types of food preservation discussed in this book are safe and will provide you and your family with convenient and nutritious food. There is no reason to fear that your food will spoil or will contain harmful contaminants. You know where your food comes from and you know the care that has gone into its preservation. And I'm going to say it again: there is no one more vested in the safety of your food than you! Not the commercial farms, not the jam-manufacturing plants, not your local grocery store.

PLANNING: YOUR KEY TO SUCCESS

With the basics under your belt, you're ready to begin. While it's possible, sometimes even necessary, to work on the spur of the moment on a food-preservation project, you'll find greater success and less stress if you plan ahead. Depending upon what you are doing, this can involve a small or large amount of investment of both time and materials.

STEP 1: WHAT AND HOW MUCH?

Decide what you want to preserve and how much you want to end up with. If you don't have enough of what you want on hand, supplement your stock (see step 2). Check out the "Fruit Yields (Canning and Freezing)" chart in the appendix for approximate yields from a specific quantity of produce to help you answer some of these "how much" questions.

Don't forget to check the recommended storage time for the product that you are storing. For example, current guidelines recommend storing canned and most frozen food for no longer than one year. This will help you decide how much to put up so that you don't run the risk of having to throw it away.

Picking your own produce at local farms and orchards can be a fun and easy way to gather the fruits and vegetables want to presserve without growing a thing yourself, or it might simply supplement your own supply. Just pick as much or as little as you need.

Farmer's markets are an amazing resource for fresh, healthy produce of all kinds. When canning and preserving, just-picked produce like this is best.

STEP 2: WHERE TO GET IT?

If you aren't growing your own fruits and vegetables, look around your area for "pick-your-own" farms or farmer's markets. Don't forget that you can negotiate; if you are buying a large quantity, be sure to ask if there's a quantity discount. As tempting as it may be, don't buy seconds or drops (produce that is not top quality or produce that has dropped to the ground). They are sure to be less expensive, but there is a greater risk of spoilage with bruised or cut produce, and older produce has already lost much of its nutritional value.

STEP 3: WHICH METHOD TO USE?

Based on what you know about the product that you want to preserve, decide which method is best. Use the safest recommended method available to you. For example, if you're going to preserve green beans and you don't have any freezer space (and you don't want pickled beans), then your choice will have to be pressure canning.

STEP 4: WHEN'S THE BEST TIME?

Try to synchronize your "canning calendar" with Mother Nature's ripening calendar. It can be tricky, but aim to schedule the time for your food-preservation project and mark it on your calendar. For example: The tomatoes are starting to ripen. Enough of them should be ripe on

Saturday to make a number of jars of stewed tomatoes, so plan to devote a few hours on Saturday afternoon to can the tomatoes. Making the time to put them up now means you'll reap great benefits later.

Just how much time you'll need depends upon the quantity of food that you are processing, how large your equipment is, and how experienced you are. If you're just starting out, plan on two to four hours. It really won't take long before you become a pro and can zip through your food-preservation projects!

Check on the fruits and vegetables in your yard often to gauge when you may need to schedule a canning day.

STEP 5: EQUIPMENT AND INGREDIENT CHECK

The instructions for each type of food preservation will give you a full list of equipment that you'll need. Likewise, each recipe will spell out the exact ingredients. Read both of these ahead of time to make sure that you have what you need on hand. Nothing is more frustrating than starting a food-preservation project and realizing that you don't have enough sugar for the jam or enough lids for the jars.

STEP 6: CONSIDER THE LOGISTICS

Check out your kitchen or other preparation area to make sure that you have enough space to work in. You don't need a commercial-size kitchen or a sanitized science laboratory. You just need a clean and uncluttered area for staging and preparation. In general, you'll need a place to gather the produce, a sink for cleaning and draining it, a place to clean and line up your storage containers (jars, lids, plastic containers, and so on) before filling, and a place to cool the processed jars. In addition, be sure to look at your long-term storage space. Do you need to make some room in the freezer or on your canning shelf?

Organizing your food and equipment before you begin helps ensure a successful and enjoyable canning experience.

STEP 7: JUST DO IT!

Your preparation is done. Now comes the fun part of actually starting your home food-preservation project. Each of the chapters to come provides step-by-step instructions, details, and recipes for:

❖ freezing

❖ water-bath and pressure canning

❖ jams, jellies, and soft spreads

❖ pickles, relishes, and salsas

INVITE A FRIEND!

In earlier times, "putting food by" was often a social affair. Folks worked together cooperatively at and after harvest to fill each other's larders. It was a time to work and a time to "gab," as my mother would call it. At the end of the day, friendships were stronger and food stores were swelled. This can work just as well today!

CHAPTER 3

Freezing: Flexible Food Preservation

Now that we have all of the background behind us, we're ready to start putting away some food. Because the goal of this book is to keep things simple, we're going to start with freezing, which is far and away the easiest and most flexible method of food preservation. Here is a short list of the advantages of freezing (one of which is that you can freeze apple rings for future pies):

❧ Freezing is the ideal first step for beginners.

❧ It's quicker, easier, and requires less preparation than canning.

❧ Food will taste better and have a better consistency than it would with most other types of food preservation.

❧ Generally, more nutrients are preserved with freezing.

❧ Food safety is less of an issue; there are no worries about botulism growing in a closed jar.

❧ It works well with a range of food: fruits and vegetables, meats and seafoods, breads and pastries, and entire meals.

❧ Almost anyone with a refrigerator/freezer and ordinary food-preparation and storage utensils can freeze food.

❧ Freezer meals are ideal for busy families—and not-so-busy families—and for folks on special diets who will want to stock up on their specialized dishes.

❧ You can easily control portion size because of the variety of storage options.

WHAT CAN YOU FREEZE?

The short, easy answer to that question is, "just about anything." Unlike other methods of food preservation, freezing doesn't depend upon eliminating or killing spoiling agents such as bacteria. If a particular food was safe to eat when you froze it and—this is very important—you keep it frozen at a steady 0 degrees Fahrenheit, it will be safe almost indefinitely. Of course, while the foods may be safe to eat, you may not want to eat them. Simply stated, some foods don't freeze well and should either only be eaten fresh or be preserved in other ways. See the sidebar "Don't Freeze These" for the short list of foods that don't freeze well. The long list of foods that *do* freeze well includes the following:

❖ Fruits

❖ Vegetables

❖ Meats and seafood

❖ Breads and pastries

❖ Meals

❖ Jams and jellies specifically formulated for freezing

❖ Almost any food stuff for which you want to extend the shelf life. For example, when your favorite orange juice is on sale, stock up and stick the half-gallons in the freezer.

We'll go into specific how-tos for each major type of food category. But first, let's look at some general guidelines and guidance.

Berries are one of the most versatile types of produce that you can freeze. Use them for pies, jellies, jams, dessert toppings, or simply as a cool snack on hot summer nights.

DON'T FREEZE THESE

Some foods don't do all that well when frozen. The list is subject to personal preference, but here are the foods I (and many others) believe become unappetizing when frozen:

❖ Salad greens and crisp raw vegetables will wilt and get soggy.

❖ Eggs in the shell will expand and crack; cooked egg whites get tough and rubbery; and meringues and icings made from egg whites get tough and weepy. The exception among eggs is the separated egg white, which does fare well.

❖ Soft dairy products (cottage cheese, whipping cream, and sour cream) and foods made from dairy, such as custard or milk sauces, will separate and become watery. Milk, however, can be successfully frozen. Just shake well after defrosting.

❖ Potatoes, when frozen raw, become mushy; when cooked or mashed, they get waterlogged and mealy.

❖ Pastas, when frozen alone for later use, get mushy and taste stale. Frozen pasta dishes, such as lasagna or macaroni and cheese, freeze reasonably well.

❖ Sandwiches generally don't freeze well. Some may differ, but I won't waste my time making and freezing most sandwiches only to have them become soggy.

❖ Except for French fries and fried onion rings, fried foods lose their crispness and get soggy.

❖ Salt loses its flavor in prepared meals.

❖ Hot and bell peppers, cloves, and artificial vanilla become strong and sometimes bitter in prepared meals.

GENERAL GUIDELINES

While in most cases freezing is as simple as putting your product into a freezer-safe container, here are some general guidelines:

❖ Use freshly picked, unblemished, fully ripe produce. The freezer is no place for second-rate, albeit bargain, products.

❖ Most vegetables must be blanched to stop enzyme action. See "All About Blanching" in the appendix for details and individual recipes for appropriate blanching times. Exceptions include vegetables used exclusively for flavoring, such as onions, peppers, and horseradish.

❖ Fruits do not need to be blanched, but light fruits should be treated to prevent darkening. See "Treating for Discoloration" in the appendix for details.

Some enzymatic processes that are harmful to flavor and nutrition need to be blanched out of vegetables before they can be frozen.

❖ Choose a freezer container suitable to the the product being frozen:

- Fruits in syrup, stews, and any food that is liquid at room temperature must be packed in a rigid container with sufficient space for expansion.
- Pack vegetables in moisture- and vapor-resistant freezer containers such as freezer bags or rigid containers.
- Wrap meats as tightly as possible in freezer wrap or butcher's paper, and secure the wrapping with freezer tape.
- Frozen meals can be put in any appropriate freezer-safe container, as long as you take care to remove excess air and seal the container completely.

❖ Label all containers—yes, including the see-through ones, even though you *know* you will remember what's in there—with the contents, amount, and "date in" and "use by" dates (for example, "1 pint green beans, sealed August 15, 2012, use by August 15, 2013").

❖ Keep an inventory of all of the food in your freezer (see the appendix for a sample). Include the item, size, date in, and date to use by, and post this on your freezer door. Unless you have a photographic memory, it's very easy to forget exactly what's in your bounty chest. It can be as simple as a hand-written piece of paper or as elaborate as a color-coded spreadsheet, but as long as you can track your consumption, you won't be caught empty-handed when that blueberry pie you were *sure* was in the freezer isn't available for a last-minute dinner party. (Be prepared to suffer a bit of teasing by folks who may find this a bit obsessive!)

❖ Check the freezer regularly to be sure that it's running and that the temperature is set at o degrees Fahrenheit. (Better safe than sorry and surrounded by spoiled food!)

❖ Twenty-four hours before freezing large amounts of food, set the thermostat back to -10 degrees Fahrenheit. This will help ensure that the new food freezes rapidly, preserving color, texture, and flavor, and helping to prevent spoilage in the case of meats and prepared meals. Once new foods are frozen, return the freezer thermostat to o degrees Fahrenheit.

❖ Cool any hot foods as quickly as possible before freezing—avoid putting hot dishes directly in the freezer. For example, after blanching vegetables, immerse them in ice water. For prepared meals, remove them from the stove and put them in a cool, clean place. I use my breezeway during the winter; we call it our "EcoFridge."

❖ Leave a little space between packages when first putting them into the freezer to allow freezing air to circulate around them. Once they freeze, push them closely together to promote freezer efficiency.

❖ Add only two to three pounds of new food for each cubic foot of freezer capacity to avoid creating unnecessary strain on the freezer motor or raising the freezer temperature.

❖ When ready to use a food, thaw it carefully using only safe thawing methods (see the sidebar below).

Thaw Safely!

Freezing is a very safe form of food preservation because the microorganisms that cause food spoilage and food-borne illness do not grow at freezing temperatures. However, these organisms are only put into a state of suspended animation! When the food is thawed, the organisms wake from their deep-frozen sleep and multiply. If not thawed properly, frozen food can be extremely dangerous; this is especially true for low-acid foods, vegetables, shellfish, and precooked dishes.

According to the US Department of Agriculture, there are three safe ways to thaw; the best is to thaw in the refrigerator. This requires planning ahead, yes, but it has more advantages than just food safety (though food safety is the best advantage!). You also save energy when you thaw in the refrigerator. The energy that was used to freeze the product is not wasted but is actually reused in your refrigerator. That is, your frozen pound of hamburger that sits in your refrigerator overnight to thaw is helping to keep your refrigerator cool, thus your refrigerator doesn't have to work so hard and uses less energy. If you put that pound of hamburger on the counter to thaw, not only are you potentially creating a safe haven for dangerous microorganisms to breed, but you are also wasting all that cold energy. In addition, foods that are thawed in the refrigerator—especially those high in water content—tend to be less mushy.

Cold-water and microwave thawing are also safe. Cold-water thawing involves, as you might guess, submerging the food in cold water. But this is more involved than it sounds. The food must be in a leak-proof package. If you get water in the food, you have two potential problems: The first is introducing bacteria into the food and therefore creating the possibility of food-borne illness. The second is water-logging the food. This may not make the food unsafe, but it will likely make it less appetizing.

To thaw food in your microwave, use the defrost setting on your microwave to safely and quickly defrost your food. Make sure you eat or cook the food immediately. Never hold partially cooked or defrosted food for any length of time. The bacteria that were present when you froze the food now have an optimal environment to grow. Because of this, never refreeze thawed food without fully cooking it to kill the bacteria.

EQUIPMENT

Except for perhaps a separate freezer, there are few things you'll need to purchase to start freezing food. Here are the basics:

❖ Freezer: chest, upright, or the freezer that's part of your refrigerator (see the next section "Freezers and Freezer Facts" that starts on page 41).

❖ Two or three large pots (at least 6- to 8-quart capacity, preferably stainless on the inside), one with a steamer insert or basket. Use these for blanching, washing, rinsing, and cooling. Do not use galvanized, copper, or iron pots because acid reacts to these metals.

❖ An assortment of bowls ranging in size from very large (more than 6 quarts) to small (1 quart) for mixing and staging

❖ Desired freezer containers (see "Freezer Containers" on page 44)

❖ Freezer or masking tape and permanent markers

❖ Large colander

❖ Cutting board

❖ Paring knife

❖ Pot holders (oven mitts)

❖ Towels, ideally absorbent cloth ones

❖ Clock or timer

THE SKINNY ON FREEZER TIME

Opinions differ about how long to store various frozen foods. In short, the less a food is processed (ground up, cooked, or seasoned), the longer it will keep in the freezer. Here's a general rule of thumb regarding storage times:

❖ Most fresh fruits and vegetables, fruit juices, and fruit jams and jellies: one year

❖ Fresh cuts of meat such as steaks, chops, and roasts (not ground) including those from beef, lamb, veal, venison, chicken, and turkey: one year

❖ Fresh pork (not ground): six to eight months

❖ Ground meats, sausages, and organ meats: three to four months

❖ Fish and shellfish: three months

❖ Cured meats (bacon, cold cuts, sausages): one month. These have a substantially shorter freezer life, because the salt reduces the freezing temperature, which can cause meat to go rancid.

❖ Prepared main dishes: one to four months

❖ Bread and pastries: less than six months

❖ Milk, ice cream, and soft cheeses: one to two months

❖ Butter and hard cheeses: six months

Note: After these suggested storage times, the frozen food won't be unsafe to eat (as long as it's been stored at the proper temperature); it just won't be very tasty or nutritious any longer.

FREEZERS AND FREEZER FACTS

When choosing and using your freezer, there are a few things to consider:

❖ **Type of freezer (chest, upright, freezer/refrigerator).** Uprights are most popular because they make it easy to see and reach all of your food. Chest freezers allow you to store more food because you can stack packages without the risk of them falling out, and they tend to be more efficient because the cold air doesn't escape as easily as it does from an upright. The freezer compartment of your refrigerator is convenient, but it is generally small and often won't keep foods as cold as a stand-alone freezer.

❖ **Size of freezer (3 cubic feet up to 25 cubic feet).** Choose the largest size that you think you will keep full. (Full freezers run more efficiently than partially full ones.) Fifteen cubic feet is good for an average family of four.

❧ **Frost-free or manual defrost.** Frost-free freezers are more convenient, but they cost more to buy and to run and can remove moisture from frozen food. Conversely, manual-defrost freezers cost less initially and are cheaper to run. Yes, you must defrost them (usually about once a year), but if you do it when the freezer is close to empty, it's not such a burdensome task—and it's a good chance to find some forgotten food treasures!

❧ **Placement.** Freezers work best in cool, dry areas such as basements and garages.

❧ **Safety (thermometers and locks).** If your freezer doesn't have a built-in thermometer, buy one at your local hardware store and check the temperature periodically to make sure your food is at a temperature no warmer than 0 degrees Fahrenheit. Locking your freezer is always a good idea, but it's a must if you have little ones around.

Because a freezer is a big investment, you might find it helpful to search the Web for some brand comparisons and recommendations.

If you have row after row of healthy fruits and vegetables in your backyard garden, and you plan to freeze them all, you'll need a stand-alone freezer.

RED ALERT! FREEZER OR POWER FAILURE

One major concern with freezing food is the potential for freezer failure because of malfunction, power outage, or simply forgetting to close the door (it happens). This is a distressing thought—especially if your freezer is full, like it should be—but take heart; in most cases, the situation's not as bad as you think. Just remember a few things: If the door has been left open, as long as the freezer continues to produce cool air, foods should be safe overnight. A full freezer should keep foods safely frozen for about two days, sometimes longer. Half full = half as long. Chest freezers stay cold longer than uprights. The freezer compartment in your refrigerator won't stay cold as long as a dedicated freezer will.

You can also take certain precautions to prevent food loss. If you are unsure of how long your freezer will be out, take one or more of the following actions, bearing in mind that you want to keep the door closed as much as possible:

❖ Add dry ice. A fifty-pound block of dry ice can keep an average full freezer at a safe temperature for three to four days. If the freezer is half full or less, that time will be reduced to two to three days. If you can't find dry ice, bagged ice is an alternative— although a less-effective one—that may keep foods safe for a day or so.

❖ If your freezer is not full, group packages together so that they retain the cold better (the same as huddling for warmth).

❖ Separate meats and poultry from other foods so that, if they do thaw, they don't contaminate other packages with their dripping juices.

❖ Ask neighbors if they have some room to spare in their freezers. If they do, pack up your wares in a cooler with ice and transport them.

Once your freezer is working again, check the freezer temperature and the temperature and condition of the food. According to the USDA, the food will be safe to eat (and can be safely refrozen) as long as it is partly frozen (still has some ice crystals) and is no warmer than 40 degrees Fahrenheit—the average temperature in your refrigerator. Unless your freezer was not working for a long time before you discovered the outage—one of the reasons for checking the temperature on a regular basis—you will probably be able to salvage most, if not all, of its contents. However, you must throw out any food that has been warmer than 40 degrees Fahrenheit for more than two hours or any food that has been touched by raw-meat fluids.

FREEZER CONTAINERS

Many years ago, when the kids were young and I wanted to try to earn a few extra coins but couldn't work days (they didn't have telecommuting back then), I sold products for a well-known plastic-container company. The gig didn't last long, but I ended up with a ton of sturdy, square freezer containers, which I would never have been able to afford. That was more than three decades ago, and I still have many of them today. The point? It's worth the investment to get good containers in which to store your frozen foods. While you *can* freeze in just about anything—plastic bags and wrap, foil, old margarine containers, carry-out containers, even the foam tray that the food was packaged in—the food will not fare as well during storage and will be less appealing when you use it. Here are some of the features you'll want to look for in your containers:

- ❧ **Sturdy.** Look for something that will last and hold up to repeated washings in your dishwasher without warping. Cheaper plastics will warp and crack.

- ❧ **Moisture- and vapor-proof.** Containers should "lock out air and lock in freshness." Sounds like a commercial, but it's true. If your containers aren't sealed well, you risk loss of moisture, which leads to freezer burn or ice-crystal formation.

- ❧ **Free from Bisphenol A (BPA).** While there's a fair amount of controversy about how safe BPA is in food storage containers, I'd stay clear of it until it's resolved. Several government agencies have issued studies and warnings about its safety.

- ❧ **Stackable and shaped suitable to the product that you're freezing.** Square and rectangular containers are the most versatile, but other shapes can come in handy for specific uses.

- ❧ **Standard and convenient sizes.** Look for freezer containers that are sized in volumes you tend to cook with (8 ounces, 16 ounces, 1 quart, 1 gallon).

- ❧ **Straight and wide.** Avoid any containers—especially glass ones—that have narrow necks at the top. If you misjudge the amount of headspace you leave, you risk cracking the container. If you want to use glass containers, stick with those that were designed to go into the freezer and have straight necks (though not recycled mayonnaise and pickle jars).

These freezer containers are especially good because they are clear, have tightly locking lids, and can be easily stacked.

Allow Sufficient Headspace

Headspace is the distance between the lid of the container and the top of the food. When liquids freeze, they expand. So for foods that have high water content, you'll need to anticipate this expansion. It won't matter as much with dry-packed fruits and vegetables, but for soups, stews, juices, and fruits packed with syrup or other liquids, headspace is important. If you don't allow sufficient space, the frozen food will pop the top off of your container. Be especially careful with soups, stews, and juices and avoid narrow-topped containers. Only use containers with tops the same width or wider than their bottoms. Foods with high water content will expand more when they freeze than those with low water content. If you put them in a narrow-topped container, they may break the container as they freeze and expand.

Use these general guidelines for headspace:

❖ Dry-packed fruits and vegetables: allow a ½-inch headspace for all containers

❖ Liquid-packed fruits and vegetables, soups, stews, juices, and so on: allow a ½-inch headspace for pints and 1 inch for quarts with wide openings. For containers with narrower openings (such as standard canning jars), leave ¾ inch for pints and 1½ inches for quarts.

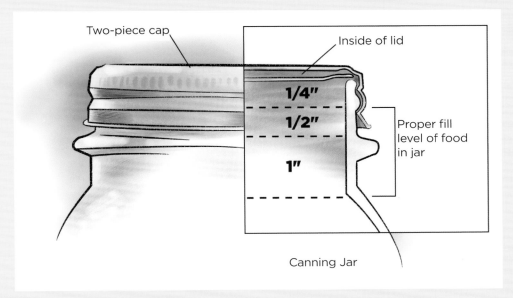

This illustration shows the kind of jar you'll use for water-bath and pressure canning, but the same principles apply to freezer containers. Keep this image in mind as you read about headspace in chapters 4 through 6.

PROCESS OVERVIEW

We'll go into specific differences between freezing fruits and vegetables in a bit, but the process is similar enough that it's worth giving you the step-by-step just once.

1. Get your produce (either picked or purchased). Look for varieties that are known to freeze well. Make sure whatever you choose is fully ripe and in great condition. If necessary, let it ripen for a few days until it's at its flavor peak.

2. If you can't freeze your produce immediately, refrigerate it.

3. Prepare your workspace. An important part of that preparation is making sure that everything is as clean as you can make it. Keep in mind that freezing doesn't kill bacteria; it just keeps them from growing.

4. For fruits only: Decide whether to dry-pack them, wet-pack them with sugar, or syrup-pack them. (I'll explain this in a bit.) This will influence the type of freezer container that you will use. All types of freezer containers are suitable for dry packing, but syrup packing works best with rigid containers—preferably ones with straight sides (not tapered) and screw-on tops.

5. For fruits only: if syrup-packing, make your syrup and let it cool (see page 50).

6. Gather and thoroughly clean all equipment and utensils.

7. Work in small quantities—just a few freezer containers at a time—to ensure the highest quality.

8. Examine and wash your produce carefully, changing the water frequently. Prepare the produce as described in the sections to follow (remove stems, seeds, and pits, and cut as desired).

9. Treat your produce to prevent darkening, if necessary. Generally, this is only for light-colored fruits such as apples, peaches, apricots, nectarines, pears, and bananas. See "Treating for Discoloration" in the appendix.

10. Blanch all vegetables as well as the fruits that you want to soften or remove skin from. (See "All About Blanching" in the appendix.)

11. Pack the produce according to instructions, leaving sufficient headspace if packing with liquid. (See "Allowing Sufficient Headspace" on page 45.)

12. Label the container with the contents and date, and update your freezer inventory.

13. Put your preserves in the freezer at -10 degrees Fahrenheit. Once the food is solidly frozen, return the freezer to 0 degrees Fahrenheit.

14. Enjoy within the next year!

THE TROUBLEMAKERS

The goal of freezing—or any type of food preservation—is to make the food not only safe but also tasty. There are a number of issues that can impair the quality of your frozen foods.

❖ **Enzymes**. Enzymes are a harmless and necessary part of life—you'll remember from earlier chapters that enzymes are chemicals found in all living organisms that control their change and growth. Unfortunately, after the product is picked, those enzymes don't understand that their job is done. They just keep working, and the changes that they inflict may not be appetizing. This can be especially noticeable in frozen foods if they have not been properly prepared. Vegetables may become tougher and more fibrous; fruits will brown and lose vitamin C. To stop the enzyme activity, simply blanch your fruits and vegetables according to the instructions in "All About Blanching" in the appendix and following the times listed in each recipe.

❖ **Freezer Burn**. Freezer burn is not a burn, but rather a loss of moisture. The dry climate inside the freezer literally saps the moisture out of frozen foods that are not sealed properly. The result depends upon the frozen product. Fruits, vegetables, breads, and meals will be dry and shriveled, often with a coating of ice crystals on the inside of the lid. Meats will take on a gray or whitish cast. In either case, the result, while not harmful, is not very appetizing and often causes loss of nutrients. Freezer burn is more likely to occur in frost-free freezers, which have fans that remove the moisture to prevent frost. This is highly preventable with the use of proper containers and wrapping methods.

❖ **Discoloration and oxidative changes**. Light-colored fruits (such as peaches, pears, apples, apricots, and bananas) begin to darken when exposed to the air. While this does not affect the safety of the food, it does make it less appetizing and less nutritious. Pretreat these to retard darkening by following the instructions in "Treating for Discoloration" in the appendix.

❖ **Mushy texture**. To ensure the best frozen product, remember to flash-freeze food at -10 degrees Fahrenheit and defrost it slowly at cool temperatures, ideally in your refrigerator.

FREEZING FRUITS

The method for freezing fruits is basically the same as described in "The Process Overview" on page 46. What changes is how you pack it, how much sugar you use, whether or not it needs to be treated to prevent darkening, and how much headspace you need to leave. With frozen fruit, the amount of sugar recommended is just that—*a recommendation*. Unlike with other types of food preservation, the safety of the fruit is not dependent upon the amount of sugar. The recipes give you recommended amounts.

PACKING THE FRUIT

You can always pack fruit dry without sugar, but many people prefer the texture and flavor of fruit that has been packed in sugar or sugar syrup. See "Sugar Syrups" on page 50 for syrup proportions.

Cookie-Sheet Quick-Freeze (CSQF) Method

To freeze flexible bulk supplies, first freeze the fruit, vegetable, or single meat portions on a large, flat sheet, such as a cookie sheet, lined with waxed or parchment paper at -10 degrees Fahrenheit. For fruits or vegetables, rinse them thoroughly, drain them, and spread them out into a single layer (for most vegetables, make sure you blanch and cool them first). For meats, pastries, breads, and so on, place single portions on the cookie sheet. Once the food is frozen, remove the cookie sheet from the freezer and quickly transfer the food to a freezer bag, making sure to break apart the frozen pieces, remove excess air, and seal the bag. (You can use rigid freezer containers, as well, but plastic zipper-style freezer bags are especially handy because they allow you to exhaust all air from inside, thus preventing freezer burn.) Any time you need some of your frozen food, simply unzip the bag, and remove only what you need—just enough blueberries for breakfast, just two chicken breasts for supper...you get the idea. Very convenient!

DRY PACKING

Dry packing is just that. After you wash and drain the fruit, treat it to prevent darkening if necessary, then put it in the container and freeze. For some fruits, such as blueberries and strawberries, the CSQF method works well (see the sidebar on page 48).

WET PACKING

For wet packing, you pack the fruit with some type of liquid, such as its own juices, sugar or honey syrup, fruit juice, crushed fruit, or water. Rigid freezer containers work best for wet-packed fruits. When packing the fruit into the container, be sure that the fruit stays covered with the juice. If necessary, pack a piece of crumpled waxed paper or plastic wrap on top of the fruit to hold it down.

❧ **Wet packing with sugar.** Sprinkle sugar (and ascorbic acid to prevent darkening, if necessary) on the fruit, and stir gently until the sugar is dissolved and the fruit's juice is drawn out.

Strawberries sprinkled with a little sugar will freeze very well. When you thaw them, the sugar will have mixed with the natural juices to form a delicious, natural syrup.

❧ **Wet packing with syrup.** Prepare a syrup by mixing the appropriate amounts of sugar and water. Depending upon what you are freezing, you may add ascorbic acid to the syrup to prevent darkening. A medium syrup (40 percent sugar) is generally good, but you might want a heavy syrup (50 percent sugar) for some tart fruits, such as sour cherries, which will benefit from the added sweetness. It will take between $\frac{1}{2}$ and $\frac{2}{3}$ cup of syrup for each pint of fruit.

Be sure to treat your peaches with ascorbic acid before freezing them so that they keep their bright yellow color.

❖ **Wet packing with fruit juice or puree**. This is a good alternative for folks who want to watch their sugar intake. Prepare a juice or puree from the less-perfect fruit (or use a commercial juice such as apple juice) and add ascorbic acid per the manufacturer's directions. Fill the container with whole, crushed, or cut fruit and cover it with the juice or puree.

Sugar Syrups

When preparing syrup packs for either canning or freezing, use the proportions below. You may use honey for part of the syrup, though it will influence the flavor of the fruit. To prepare the syrup, combine the ingredients in a pan and bring them to a boil. Simmer the mixture until the sugar is completely dissolved. Depending upon the syrup's intended use, either cool it or use it while hot. You will need approximately ½ to ⅔ cups of syrup for each pint and 1 to 1½ cups for each quart that you can.

TYPE OF SYRUP	PERCENTAGE OF SUGAR	CUPS OF SUGAR	CUPS OF HONEY	CUPS OF WATER	YIELD IN CUPS OF SYRUP
Extra-light	20	1½	0	5½	6
Light	30	2¼	0	5¼	6½
Medium	40	3¼	0	5	7
Heavy	50	4¼	0	4¼	7
Honey	0	0	1	4	5

Frozen Fruit Recipes

Here are details for freezing some of your favorite fruits. For those that require treatment for darkening, follow the directions in "Treating for Discoloration" in the appendix. **Before processing any fruit, wash it, remove any stems and pits, and drain or dry it; follow the individual instructions for each recipe, then seal, label, and put the container in the freezer.**

Apples Slices or Rings

1. Make a heavy syrup, including treatment for discoloration.
2. Put ½ cup of syrup in each freezer container.
3. Add fruit to fill the container, press it down, and add more syrup to cover it, leaving the appropriate headspace (see page 45).

Apple Slices or Rings for Pie

1. Pretreat slices to prevent darkening, then pack the apples into a plastic freezer bag.
2. Put the bag into a pie plate so that it takes the plate's shape while freezing.
3. Once the slices are frozen, remove the pie plate.
4. When you're ready to use the apples, prepare your pastry and line the pie plate.
5. Remove the frozen apples from the bag, place them directly into the pastry, add sugar and spices, and bake as directed.

Applesauce

1. Make applesauce according to your favorite recipe, or see the recipe on page 88.
2. Cool the applesauce and ladle it into containers, leaving the appropriate headspace.

Soft Berries (Raspberries, Blackberries...)—Whole

- **To dry-pack:** you can freeze the berries normally or use the CSQF method (see page 48).
- **To sugar-pack:** Use 1 part sugar to 4 parts berries.
- **To syrup-pack:** Make a heavy syrup. Put the fruit in your container, shake it to settle the fruit, and then cover the fruit with syrup, leaving the appropriate headspace.

Firm Berries (Blueberries, Huckleberries...)—Whole

❖ **To dry-pack:** You can freeze the berries normally or use the CSQF method.

❖ **To sugar-pack:** Mix ²/₃ cup sugar per quart of fruit.

❖ **To syrup-pack:** Make a heavy syrup. Put the fruit in your container, shake it to settle the fruit, and then cover the fruit with syrup, leaving the appropriate headspace.

Cherries—Sour, Whole

❖ **To sugar-pack:** Use 1 part sugar to 4 parts cherries.

❖ **To syrup-pack:** Make a heavy syrup. Put the fruit in a container, shake the container to settle the fruit, and cover the fruit with syrup, leaving the appropriate headspace.

Cherries—Sweet, Whole

1. Make a heavy syrup that includes treatment for discoloration.

2. Pack the cherries into a container, shake it to settle the fruit, and cover the fruit with syrup, leaving the appropriate headspace.

Cranberries—Whole

Cranberries are easy: just dry-pack them in a container leaving a ½-in. headspace. You can also use the CSQF method.

Fruit Juices

Here's another easy one: Ladle juice into freezer jars or plastic freezer containers, leaving the appropriate headspace. See chapter 4 for recipes to make your own juice.

Peaches, Nectarines, and Apricots—Sliced or Halved

If you like, you can blanch the fruit for 30 to 60 seconds to remove the skin before slicing. (See "All About Blanching" in the appendix.) Add treatment for discoloration to either pack.

❖ **To sugar-pack:** Coat each quart of sliced fruit with ²/₃ cup sugar and let the fruit stand for 10 minutes before packing it in freezer containers, leaving the appropriate headspace.

❖ **To syrup-pack:** Make a heavy syrup. Ladle ½ cup of syrup into freezer jars or plastic freezer containers, fill them with sliced fruit, shake gently to settle, and cover the fruit with syrup, leaving the appropriate headspace.

Pears—Sliced or Halved

1. Make a medium syrup and add a treatment for discoloration.

2. Bring the syrup to a boil, add pears (sliced or halved), and cook them for 2 minutes.

3. Cool the pears in the syrup, and pack the mixture into freezer containers, leaving the appropriate headspace.

Rhubarb—Cut into 1-inch Slices

Although technically a vegetable, you can freeze rhubarb like you would fruits that don't need blanching.

❖ **To dry pack:** Put the slices directly into the desired container. You can also use the CSQF method.

❖ **To sugar pack:** Coat the fruit with 1 part sugar for every 4 parts rhubarb, let it stand until the sugar dissolves, and then pack the mixture into freezer containers, leaving the appropriate headspace.

❖ **To syrup pack:** Make a heavy syrup. Place the fruit into freezer jars or plastic containers and cover with syrup, leaving the appropriate headspace.

Strawberries—Whole or Sliced Lengthwise

❖ **To dry-pack:** Place the fruit in the desired container, leaving a 1/2-inch headspace. You can also use the CSQF method.

❖ **To sugar-pack:** Mix 1 part sugar to 6 parts fruit and let it stand until the sugar is dissolved, stirring gently. Pack the mixture into containers, leaving the appropriate headspace.

FREEZING VEGETABLES

Freezing is a favorite way to preserve your garden's bounty of vegetables because it is simple and safe. Because vegetables are low in acid, you have only one canning option: pressure-canning to prevent spoilage and food poisoning. Freezing is quicker and easier (the steps are very similar to those for freezing fruit). One major difference is that vegetables always require blanching to stop enzyme action.

Frozen Veggie Recipes

Here are details for freezing some of your favorite veggies. The blanching times given are for boiling-water blanching. If steam-blanching, add one to two minutes to the given time (unless stated otherwise). For most vegetables, using the CSQF (see page 48) technique is a great way to produce flexible supplies of your favorite food. **For all recipes, wash the vegetables thoroughly, prepare them as instructed, blanch them, cool them quickly, drain or dry them thoroughly, and pack them into containers, leaving a ½-inch headspace; then seal, label, and freeze them.**

Asparagus

1. Trim the stalks to remove the woody ends, sort them by size, and cut them into even lengths to fit into the containers.
2. Blanch small spears for 2 minutes and large spears for 3 minutes.
3. Cool, then pack the cut and blanched asparagus into containers leaving *a ½-inch headspace*.

You can also use the CSQF method after blanching.

A HANDY SUPPLY OF BELL PEPPERS AND ONIONS

Save time with food preparation throughout the winter with a handy supply of vegetables, such as peppers and onions, to use for flavoring. Vegetables that are just used for flavoring do not need to be blanched like other vegetables do. For example, chop up green or red peppers to the size that you would normally use in your recipes—probably ¼-inch squares—and freeze them, with a little space between each, on a cookie sheet lined with waxed paper. Once they are frozen hard, store them in a freezer container or zipper-style freezer bag. When you need that quarter cup of chopped peppers for your pasta sauce, simply take out what you need and return the rest to the freezer.

Beans—Lima

1. Select young beans (seeds should still be green, not turning yellow), wash them in cold water, shell them, and wash them again.

2. Separate the beans by size and blanch them: 1 minute for small ones, 2 minutes for medium ones, and 3 minutes for large ones.

3. Cool, then pack the beans into containers, leaving a ½-inch headspace.

You can also use the CSQF method after blanching.

Beans—Green, Hull, Italian, Purple, Snap, or Wax

1. Select young, tender bean pods.

2. Wash them in cold water, trim the ends, and cut as desired (2–4-inch sections work well, or slice lengthwise for French-cut beans).

3. Blanch the beans for 3 minutes.

4. Cool, then pack them into containers, leaving a ½-inch headspace.

You can also use the CSQF method after blanching.

Beets

1. Select uniform, tender beets.

2. Cut their stems to 2 inches long and leave the taproots.

3. Cook the beets whole until they are tender. Cool them and then remove their stems, skins, and taproots. You can leave the beets whole or quarter, slice, or dice them.

4. Cool, then pack the beets into containers, leaving a ½-inch headspace.

You can also use the CSQF method after blanching.

Broccoli

1. Select young, tender stalks.

2. Wash and remove the leaves and woody stalks. Cut the broccoli into sections of desired size.

3. Soak the sections for 30 minutes in brine (use 1 cup of salt to 1 gallon of water) to kill any insects. (Skim them off as they float to the surface of the water.)

4. Blanch the broccoli for 2 to 4 minutes, depending upon size; it'll turn bright green when it's done.

5. Cool, then pack the sections into containers, leaving a ½-inch headspace.

You can also use the CSQF method after blanching.

Brussels Sprouts

1. Select sprouts with dark-green, compact heads.
2. Remove them from their stalks, remove the rough outer leaves, and sort the sprouts by size.
3. Blanch them: 3 minutes for small ones, 4 minutes for medium ones, and 5 minutes for large ones.
4. Cool, then pack like-sized sprouts into containers, leaving a 1/2-inch headspace.

You can also use the CSQF method after blanching.

Carrots

1. Select young, tender, coreless, medium-length carrots.
2. Wash and peel the carrots, and then wash them again. You can leave the carrots whole, or you can dice or quarter them.
3. Blanch cut carrots for 3 minutes and whole carrots for 5 minutes.
4. Cool, then pack them into containers, leaving a 1/2-inch headspace.

You can also use the CSQF method after blanching.

Cauliflower

1. Select compact heads.
2. Trim them and break or cut them into uniform 1-inch flowerets.
3. Wash, drain, and then soak them for 30 minutes in brine (1 cup salt to 1 gallon water) to kill any insects. (Skim them off as they float to the surface of the water.)
4. Blanch the cauliflower: 3 minutes for medium heads and 4 minutes for large ones.
5. Cool, then pack them into containers, leaving a 1/2-inch headspace.

You can also use the CSQF method after blanching.

Corn—Cream Style

1. Select tender, freshly picked corn; husk the ears and remove any silk.
2. Blanch the cobs for 4 minutes and then cool them.
3. Cut the kernels off the cobs, leaving the small kernels at the tips. For creamier corn, cut at the center of the kernels, leaving the bottom halves of the kernels on the cobs.
4. Scrape the cobs with a knife to squeeze out the pulp and milk. Add this to the cut corn and stir to combine.
5. Pack the corn, pulp, and milk mixture into containers, leaving a 1/2-inch headspace.

Corn—Whole Kernel

Frozen corn on the cob rarely matches the experience of fresh corn on the cob and can be disappointing. The best way to freeze corn is to freeze it after it has been cut (you can use the CSQF method).

1. Select tender, freshly picked corn; husk the corn, trim it, and remove any silk.
2. Blanch the corn for 4 minutes and then cool it.
3. Cut the kernels off the cobs, leaving the small kernels at the tip. Do not scrape the cob.
4. Pack the kernels into containers, leaving a 1/2-inch headspace.

Eggplant

1. Select dark, young eggplant (before the seeds are large and mature).
2. Working quickly to avoid darkening, prepare (wash, peel, and slice 1/3-inch thick) only enough eggplant for one blanching batch.
3. Blanch the eggplant for 4 minutes in a solution of 1 gallon of water with either 1/3 cup of lemon juice or 3 tablespoons of ascorbic acid. Cool and drain.
4. Pack in containers with food-grade plastic wrap separating individual slices.

You can also use the CSQF method after blanching.

Greens—Swiss Chard, Collards, Kale, Spinach

1. Select young, tender leaves.
2. Wash the greens thoroughly, taking care—especially with chard—to remove all soil; remove woody or tough stems.
3. Blanch the greens: 3 minutes for collard and 2 minutes for chard, kale, and spinach.
4. Cool, and pack them into containers, leaving a 1/2-inch headspace.

Herbs—Fresh

Use frozen herbs in cooked dishes—not as garnish (because they will be limp).

1. Gently wash, drain, and pat the herbs dry. Do not blanch them.
2. Wrap single portions in food-grade plastic wrap, and place the wrapped portions in a plastic freezer bag.

You can also use the CSQF method.

Mushrooms—Steamed or Sautéed

1. Use cultivated mushrooms that are fresh and free of spots or decay.

2. Wash the mushrooms thoroughly in cold water. Trim the ends of the stems. If the mushrooms are larger than 1 inch across, slice or quarter them.

3. Steam or sauté the mushrooms in butter, margarine, or olive oil. Steamed mushrooms last longer. Steam whole, button, or quartered mushrooms for 9 minutes, and steam slices for 5 minutes.

   ❖ **For steamed only:** Dip the mushrooms for 5 minutes in a solution of 2 cups water and 1 teaspoon of lemon juice or 1½ teaspoons of citric acid. Drain them, then steam and drain them again. Cool, then pack them into containers.

   ❖ **For sautéed only:** Heat small amounts of the mushrooms in butter, margarine, or olive oil and cook them until they are almost done. Cool, then pack them into containers.

Peas—Green

1. Select pods with young, tender peas (before they have become starchy).

2. Wash and shell the peas, and then wash them again.

3. Blanch the peas for 2 minutes.

4. Cool, then pack the peas into containers, leaving a ½-inch headspace.

You can also use the CSQF method after blanching.

Peas—Edible Pod (Snow or Sugar Snap)

1. Choose young, firm, unblemished pods. You want to get them before the peas have fully matured.

2. Wash them and snip their ends, if necessary.

3. Blanch the peas for 2 minutes.

4. Cool, then pack them into containers, leaving a ½-inch headspace.

You can also use the CSQF method after blanching.

Peppers—All Types

When handling hot peppers, or sometimes even red bell peppers, wear gloves to protect your hands from potential burning. For both hot and sweet peppers: select crisp, tender green or red fruit; wash and drain it—do not blanch it.

❖ **For hot peppers:** Pack whole into plastic freezer containers, leaving no headspace.

❖ **For sweet peppers:** Pack whole, halved, sliced, or chopped into containers, leaving a 1/2-inch headspace.

You can also use the CSQF method for these.

Pumpkin and Winter Squash

Do not blanch pumpkins or squash, but cook them completely (see preparation details). Pumpkins and winter squash store well in a cool, dry place but can also be very convenient when pureed and frozen.

1. Select fully ripe pumpkins and winter squash with hard rinds and stringless, mature meat.
2. Wash and halve them; place them cut-side down in a baking dish filled with 1/4 inch of water, cover the dish loosely, and bake at 375 degrees Fahrenheit until the pumpkin or squash is tender, about 60 minutes.
3. Cool the pumpkin or squash, drain it if necessary, scoop out the flesh, and mash or puree it. Pack the puree into containers, leaving a 1/2-inch headspace.

If using the pumpkin or squash for pie, drain it well; add 1 part sugar to 6 parts puree, if desired. Measure the amount necessary for the pie recipe. Then pack it into containers, leaving a 1/2-inch headspace.

Summer Squash

Frozen summer squash is limp and watery; plan to use it for casseroles rather than for side dishes.

1. Choose young, tender squash (before the seeds have fully matured).
2. Wash it, cut off the ends, and slice it.
3. Blanch the squash for 3 minutes.
4. Cool, then pack the sliced squash into containers, leaving a 1/2-inch headspace.

Tomatoes—Raw

Use frozen tomatoes only for cooking because they will be soft when thawed.

1. Select firm, ripe tomatoes.

2. Wash the tomatoes, then blanch them for 30 seconds to remove the skins. Cut out the stem ends. Leave the tomatoes whole or cut them into pieces.

3. Cool, then pack them into containers, leaving a ½-inch headspace.

Tomato Juice or Sauce

Do not blanch tomatoes used for juice or sauce. Cook them according to the preparation details.

1. Select firm, ripe plum or Italian-style tomatoes.

2. Wash them, cut them into even-size pieces, and simmer the pieces in a heavy pan for 5 to 10 minutes, adding only enough water to keep from sticking.

3. Press the cooked pieces through a sieve or food mill; add 1 teaspoon of salt per quart of juice, if desired.

   ❧ If making juice, cool and pour it into freezer jars, leaving the appropriate headspace (see page 45).

   ❧ If making sauce, return it to the heavy pan and cook it down to the desired consistency. Cool and pour it into freezer jars, leaving the appropriate headspace.

Tomatoes—Stewed

1. Select firm, ripe tomatoes.

2. Wash them, blanch them for 30 seconds, slip off the skins, cut out their stem ends, and quarter them.

3. Place the quartered tomatoes in a heavy pan, cover it, and cook until they're tender (10 to 20 minutes). Cool the tomatoes quickly by placing the pan in ice water. Remove the pan when cooled, scoop out the tomatoes, and pack them into containers, leaving a ½-inch headspace.

AND DON'T OVERLOOK FREEZING...

As I said earlier, you can freeze anything safely, but not all items freeze well. So far, I have focused on the more common items you can freeze (fruits, vegetables, meat/poultry/seafood, and prepared meals). Here's a snapshot of some of the other foods that can be conveniently and safely frozen.

JAMS AND SAUCES

If you want to make jams but don't want to take the time to can them using a water-bath canner, there are many types of freezer jam that you can make in minutes—really! I like them better than the canned variety because they have a much fresher taste (they don't need to be cooked as long as conventional jams). Check out chapter 5 for more recipes, but below is one for my daughter Katie's favorite: strawberry freezer jam. Freezer jams will safely keep for a year.

Strawberry Freezer Jam

This jam is simply too easy and too good! I used to make it with my children when they were just toddlers. If you don't want to freeze the whole recipe, the jam will keep in the refrigerator for about two to four weeks—but it won't last that long!

Yield: 2½ pints

Ingredients:

❖ 1 quart strawberries, crushed to make 2 cups

❖ 4 cups sugar—do not adjust

❖ 1 (1.75 ounce) package of regular-style, dry powdered pectin

❖ ¾ cup water

If you freeze in rigid containers, it's very important to leave enough headspace for the jam to expand.

1. Clean and sterilize the freezer containers or freezer jars. Half-pint (8-ounce) containers are a good size for this.

2. Mix crushed strawberries with sugar and let stand for 10 minutes.

3. While waiting, stir the pectin into the water in a small saucepan. Bring to a boil over medium-high heat; boil for 1 minute.

4. Stir the boiling water into the strawberry/sugar mixture. Stir for 3 minutes. (It's okay if a few sugar crystals remain.)

5. Pour into prepared containers, leaving a ½-inch headspace.

6. Place tops on the containers, and let them sit at room temperature for 24 hours. Place into freezer and store frozen until ready to use.

Frozen muffins are almost as good as freshly baked ones! When baking muffins, double the batch and squirrel away a few extras for later in the month.

BREADS, CAKES, AND PASTRIES

They are always handy to have on hand, but baked goods have a shorter shelf life than fruits and vegetables and can be more of a challenge to wrap well because of their size and shape. Here are a few things to consider:

❖ For all baked products, cool them first before putting them into the freezer.

❖ Wrap as tightly as possible. Bread frozen in the store wrapper is likely to either get freezer burn (dry out) or be soggy from ice crystals inside the wrapper. A good way to handle baked goods is to first freeze them unwrapped, then wrap the frozen product tightly.

❖ You can freeze yeast breads unbaked, baked, or as brown-and-serve.

❖ You can freeze baked cookies or cookie dough. For baked cookies, follow the instructions for all baked products. If freezing drop cookies, use the CSQF (see page 48) technique to freeze individual cookies, then just thaw what you need to bake and keep the rest in the freezer for another day!

DAIRY AND EGGS

Of course, everyone freezes ice cream, sherbets, and sorbets, but other dairy products—including eggs—can also be successfully frozen. The freezer life of eggs is shorter than that of fruits and vegetables, so be sure to note the dates on the label. Always thaw dairy and eggs in the refrigerator—never at room temperature. Here are a few things to remember:

❖ **Eggs.** Use only the freshest eggs. Do not freeze them in their shells. Freeze egg whites and yolks together, or separate them into just whites or just yolks.

- For freezing both whites and yolks and for just whites: mix them gently without forming air bubbles. A sieve or colander is helpful here to separate the yolk from the white. Put the mixture in a freezer container, leaving a ½-inch of headspace.

- For freezing yolks: mix them gently and add 1½ teaspoons of sugar or ⅛ teaspoon of salt for every four yolks. This will help prevent them from becoming gelatinous when frozen. Be sure to mark the container so that you choose the right flavor for your dish (sugar with sweet dishes and salt with savory ones).

❖ **Butter.** Use fresh, high-quality butter from pasteurized cream. Freeze in sticks or in the desired shape using the CSQF method. Freezing is very handy for making decorative butter pats.

❖ **Cheese.** The harder the cheese, the better it will take to freezing and the longer it will keep. Soft cheeses, such as cottage cheese or ricotta, work especially well if you're planning to use them in a baked dish, such as lasagna.

❖ **Cream.** If it's at least 40 percent butterfat, you can freeze it, but it's really not worth the effort. You need to heat it to 170 degrees Fahrenheit and add 3 teaspoons of sugar to each pint to help prevent it from separating. Even then, it's highly susceptible to picking up flavors in the freezer.

You'll find it very convenient to have a back-up supply of butter or grated cheese in your freezer.

Take advantage of sales at your local butcher to stock up on cuts of meat that you might otherwise pass by. Beef steaks, chops, and roasts freeze well. Freeze individual steaks or chops using the CSQF (see page 48) method for real convenience!

MEATS

As with food in other categories, freezing has become the method of choice for preserving meats and poultry because it retains the natural fresh qualities of the meat and is quick, easy, and safe. Store all cuts of meat in tightly wrapped packages to avoid freezer burn. How you plan to use your meat will determine the best packaging.

❖ Roasts, hamburger, whole and half chickens and turkeys, and other large cuts: Wrap them tightly. Roasts and large cuts work best when wrapped in freezer wrap, freezer foil, or plastic freezer bags. Hamburger and ground meats can be stored conveniently in plastic containers, provided they are filled to within $\frac{1}{2}$ inch of the top to avoid excess air in the container.

❖ Steaks, chops, individual hamburger patties, or cut-up chicken and turkey: Wrap them individually or use the CSQF (see page 48) method and store in a plastic freezer bag. This will allow you to take out just the cuts you want for one meal.

Follow these steps to ensure safe storage of any meat:

1. If freezing a large amount of meat, such as a quarter of beef, set your freezer back to -10 degrees Fahrenheit twenty-four hours ahead of time.

2. Before beginning, make sure the preparation area, utensils, and storage containers are clean.

3. Set up a staging area so that you can work quickly, ensuring that meats stay cold during wrapping. The only equipment that you should need is a sharp knife (if you plan to trim or divide any of the cuts), freezer wrap or containers, freezer tape, and a marker.

4. Decide which cuts (such as roasts) you will want to freeze whole, and which cuts you would like to quick-freeze using the CSQF method.

5. Work in small batches, wrapping and freezing one batch before beginning another. This helps ensure that the meat will stay cold and safe.

6. Wrap as desired and mark the outside with the item's name, date frozen, and date to use by. (See suggested storage times in the sidebar "The Skinny on Freezer Time" on page 41.)

7. Place the cuts in the freezer immediately, separating the packages slightly to allow for the circulation of cold air.

8. Once the meat is frozen solid, return the thermostat to 0 degrees Fahrenheit and push the packages together to promote freezer efficiency.

9. Enjoy the meat before the expiration date. While most meats are safe for a year, cured meats, sausages, and ground meats have a shorter shelf life in the freezer.

10. When thawing, always use safe thawing methods (see the sidebar "Thaw Safely!" on page 39). Thawing in the refrigerator is best. Never—*ever*—thaw poultry at room temperature because of the risk of salmonella.

SEAFOOD AND CURED PORK

Seafood can be frozen, but it is more susceptible to bacterial contamination and spoilage, and it has a significantly shorter shelf life. If you are interested if preserving a large quantity of seafood (maybe you had a great day on the boat), refer to more specialized resources for guidance.

Cured pork—ham, bacon, and other cured cuts with a high salt content—don't fare well in the freezer. They quickly lose their desirable flavor and color. They can be frozen safely, but plan to use them much sooner than other cuts of meat (within a month) for best results. Store all cuts in tightly wrapped packages to avoid freezer burn.

When everyone's gone home after a big Thanksgiving meal, package up those leftovers and stick them in the freezer to enjoy again another day.

FREEZER MEALS

If having fruits, vegetables, meats, and breads at your fingertips is a great convenience and cost savings, the next best thing is having entire meals waiting for you to use. It's like having a "Drive-Thru" in your basement, and it's all those things that most fast food generally is not: nutritious, locally grown, chemical free, and free of hydrogenated oils and high-fructose corn syrup. You know what's in the meal that you pull from the freezer because you made it with your own ingredients.

There are a few key points to remember when creating freezer meals:

❖ Keep storage times in mind. Prepared foods have a shorter shelf life in the freezer than unprepared foods do—three to six months versus eight to twelve months. In your zeal to maximize your time, don't cook and freeze more than you can realistically eat.

❖ Stick with one type of meal per container rather than attempting to create your own version of a TV dinner. Different foods have different thaw and cook times, and you don't want to end up with your meat perfect but your vegetables incinerated.

❖ Test-drive a single meal of a new recipe before you invest in an eight-meal mega cook-a-thon only to find that your family hates it.

❖ Consider teaming up with friends or family members to share the work and the food.

Baby Food Shortcut

Tired of spending so much money and wasting so much packaging on baby food? Worried about what's in the food? Does your baby have special dietary needs? If you answered "yes" to any of these questions, you can easily make your own baby food and then conveniently freeze meal-size portions in small containers. One of the easiest methods is to fill plastic ice cube trays (BPA-free ones, of course) and freeze the food; then remove the individual food blocks, stack them in conveniently sized, airtight containers separated by waxed paper or foil, and keep them in your freezer. When you need a serving, remove one or two cubes and thaw them in either the refrigerator or the microwave.

Baby Eleanor's Sweet Potatoes

Sweet potatoes were one of the earliest solid foods introduced to my granddaughter Eleanor. She loved them. Here's her mom, Katie's, recipe for keeping a convenient and economical supply handy.

1. Wash and peel the sweet potatoes or yams.

2. Cut them into cooking-sized pieces (slices about $\frac{1}{2}$-inch thick), and place them in a saucepan. Add just enough water to keep them from burning. Bring everything to a boil and let it simmer gently for about 20 minutes, until soft.

3. Mash the cooked sweet potatoes or yams well—or better yet, blend them using an immersion blender or food processor for baby-smooth consistency.

4. Cool, and feed one portion to the baby. Pack the remainder in portion-size freezer containers. Make sure you label and date the containers before freezing.

5. To use a portion, take it out the day before you expect to use it and thaw it in the refrigerator. If you forget, thaw it in microwave.

CHAPTER 4

Canning: A Fresh Take on a Favorite Pastime

Canning, now also known by the trendy term *fresh preserving*, is enjoying a renaissance, and rightfully so. People are rediscovering an art that has too-long been ignored. We're learning, as you'll see shortly, that canning is not nearly as complicated as its reputation might suggest. In fact, it's possible to water-bath can 7 quarts of peaches in not much more time than you would spend making a peach pie. We covered many of the benefits of home canning in the first chapters, but here are a few highlights:

❖ **Sustainability.** Jars and bands are often a one-time investment and can be reused year after year, as long as they remain in good condition (no chips).

❖ **Economy.** The energy involved to can and keep food is low. Once canned and sealed, jars do not need to be frozen or refrigerated.

❖ **Ease of storage.** Unlike frozen foods, you can store canned goods almost anywhere, so your storage space is limitless.

❖ **Convenience.** There is no need to thaw food; it's always ready to use—just pry open the lid, cook, and serve.

❖ **Nutrition.** Because fruits and vegetables lose their nutrients rapidly after being picked, a jar of canned fruits or vegetables is likely to be higher in nutrients than "fresh" fruit that has been stored or transported for several weeks to your local grocery store.

WHAT CAN YOU CAN?

While the list of foods suitable for canning isn't quite as extensive as the one for freezing, it pretty much excludes only baked goods and dairy. The most popular home-canned products are fruits, tomatoes and tomato sauces, jams and jellies, salsas and savory spreads, and pickles and relishes, which are all high-acid foods and can be canned using boiling water (water-bath canning). But don't overlook the convenience of canning vegetables, meats, soups, and stews, which are all low-acid and thus require the higher temperatures of pressure canning.

HIGH- AND LOW-ACID CANNING

Back in chapter 2, when we were looking at all the things that can go wrong (but won't, because you're reading this book), we talked about a fundamental principle in canning—the treatment of high-acid versus low-acid foods. If you skipped that chapter, it's worth taking a minute to look at "How Acid and Heat Work Together in Food Preservation" on page 25. To summarize briefly:

❖ **High-acid foods** (most fruits, pickled products, jams, jellies, salsas, and tomatoes) have a built-in defense (acid) against many microorganisms and can be safely preserved by a process called water-bath canning.

Canned tomatoes are easy to process and are a real "utility player" in the kitchen. Use them for pasta sauce, meat loaf, soups, stews, and more.

❖ **Low-acid foods** (most vegetables, some tomatoes, meats, fish, and poultry) do not have sufficient acid to keep harmful microorganisms at bay and—be sure to write this down or tattoo it onto your hand—*they must be preserved using a process called pressure canning*.

Both types of canning involve similar basic steps, which we'll discuss in depth in a moment. But for now, suffice it to say that you put the prepared food into jars, close with lids and bands, and put the jars in either a big kettle with boiling water (water-bath canning) or in a specially designed sealed pot that creates pressurized steam (pressure canning). In both cases, you cook the jars and their contents for the time specified in the recipe. This cooking accomplishes two important things: it kills the microorganisms that could cause spoilage, and it creates an airtight seal that prevents new microorganisms from entering the jar.

I'll give you more information about these two different types of canning, how to choose the right method for your needs, and what equipment you'll need, plus step-by-step instructions and some help if things don't go according to plan.

GETTING READY

This may sound familiar because it's true of all types of food preservation: planning ahead will help make your canning experience fun and gratifying and your canned foods tasty, nutritious, and safe. Especially when you're first getting started, you'll want to allow yourself enough time so that you don't need to rush. Unlike the recipes for freezing foods, which are based on taste preferences and maintaining the highest-quality texture and flavor, the recipes for canning food have been carefully tested by food-safety experts, such as those at the United States Department of Agriculture (USDA), to ensure that the food is safe to eat when you open the jar. This book gives you all the instructions that you'll need for basic recipes and should serve your canning needs for many seasons. When you outgrow this book, there are lots of other really good guides that have safe and delicious recipes (see Resources).

PLAYING IT SAFE

Home canning is perfectly safe, as long as you:

❖ Use only top-quality, blemish-free food

❖ Follow instructions exactly

❖ Use only up-to-date equipment

❖ Do not use any recipes created before 1988. If you have heirloom recipes from Grandma, take them to your local agricultural extension service and ask them to review and adjust them.

Any convenience added by cutting corners is not worth the risk of food spoilage, or worse, food poisoning, or much worse, food poising from botulism. While it is very rare, *Clostridium botulinum*, the deadly bacterium that causes botulism, thrives in under-processed, low-acid, canned goods. This nasty bug is very potent and very deadly. Better safe than sorry!

If you want the perfect peach preserves, you'll have to begin with the perfect peaches.

In the appendix are charts to help you with the planning, including helping you approximate how much produce to buy or pick at one time. In my experience, it's really hard to look at a bushel of apples and imagine that you could ever use that many. But when you realize that bushel will later manifest as about 14 quarts of applesauce—a little over one quart a month—it doesn't seem like so much.

Here are a few questions to ask yourself as you get ready:

❖ What do you want to can?

❖ Where will you get it?

❖ When will you can it?

❖ How will you can it? See the sidebar "Water-Bath Versus Pressure Canning" for help deciding.

❖ Do you have the equipment that you need? (The next section goes into details about the supplies that you'll need for canning. It's really pretty inexpensive.)

❖ Do you have a tested recipe, and do you understand it? If you're using the recipes in this book, you'll know that they are all tested and safe, and (I hope) easy to follow. If you're not using the provided recipes, and you have any concern about whether a recipe of your own is tested and safe, contact your local Cooperative Extension Service.

❖ Do you have all of the ingredients needed? If the recipe calls for water or salt, use soft or distilled water and canning/pickling salt. The minerals in hard water and the additives in some table salt can cause the liquid in your canned product to become cloudy—this isn't harmful, but it is a bit unappetizing.

Your small investment in equipment will quickly be returned as you enjoy your bounty of tasty canned goods.

EQUIPMENT

If you are new to canning, you can get up and running with a fairly minimal investment. The equipment falls into the following categories: canners; utensils; jars, lids, and bands; and normal kitchen supplies.

CANNERS

As we've mentioned before, there are two basic types of canners: water-bath canners for high-acid foods, and pressure canners for low-acid foods. Both work like your other kitchen stockpots, heating the water on your stovetop. They are very large covered kettles (we'll use the words *kettle* and *pot* interchangeably), with oversized, flat bottoms. Before you invest in a large canner, make sure that your stovetop can accommodate it. The canner you choose should be no more than 4 inches in diameter larger than the diameter of your burner (with an overhang of 2 inches on either side). Traditional electric coil stovetops require flat-bottomed pots, while gas burners can accommodate either flat-bottomed or ridged pots. Some of the new cook surfaces, such as convection or ceramic, may not be suitable for such large pots. Be sure to check your stovetop manufacturer's recommendations to be sure that your canner is compatible with your stovetop.

Water-Bath Versus Pressure Canning

Here's how water-bath canning differs from pressure canning:

- **Water-bath canning** involves processing jars in *boiling water*, which at sea level, reaches a temperature of *212 degrees Fahrenheit*, sufficient to kill all molds and yeasts, as well as *some bacteria*. You use a large covered pot (canner) that has a rack to keep the jars off the bottom of the pot and away from each other.
- **Pressure canning** involves processing jars in *pressurized steam*, which at sea level, reaches a temperature of *240 degrees Fahrenheit*, sufficient to kill all molds and yeasts, *and all bacteria and bacterial spores*. You use a specially designed pressure canner, which is capable of forming a tight seal and thus raising the pressure of the steam within.

The chart below tells you when you should use water-bath canning and when you should use pressure canning.

FOOD	WATER-BATH CANNING	PRESSURE CANNING	COMMENTS
Fruits	YES	YES	Water-bath canning is the logical choice, but pressure canning can be used for some fruits. (See the appendix.) Figs are borderline in acidity. For them, use only recipes that add acid to lower the pH.
Jams, jellies, salsas	YES	NO	See chapter 5, but generally jams, jellies, and salsas are high-acid and easily processed by water-bath canning.
Meat products, stews, soups, and so on	NO	YES	You must use pressure canning, as well as tested and approved recipes, when canning anything with meat.
Tomatoes	YES, see comments	YES	Some new hybrids, as well as overly ripe tomatoes, can be marginal in their acidity. Most water-bath canning recipes will call for adding acid (usually bottled lemon or citric acid).
Tomato sauce, tomato juice, stewed tomatoes, or other combinations of tomatoes with low-acid vegetables	YES, see comments	YES	Follow recipes carefully to ensure that you maintain the proportions and therefore the acid level. For example, if you increase the amount of onion, pepper, or garlic, the overall acidity may fall and the pH level may rise above 4.6—the measurement for low-acid foods.
Vegetables	NO	YES	When you think of vegetables, such as corn, beans, or peas, *you must think pressure canning!* That is the only safe option. Use only tested and approved recipes.

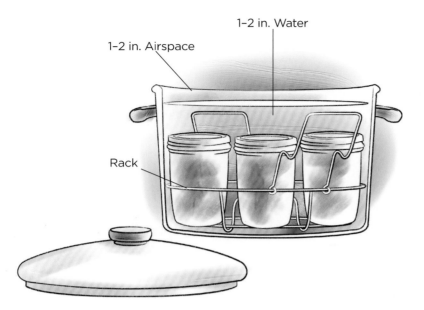

1–2 in. Airspace

1–2 in. Water

Rack

Standard canners are tall enough so that you can cover the jars with 2 inches of water and still have 2 inches of headspace above the boiling water.

WATER-BATH CANNERS

There are a number of sizes and styles of water-bath canners to choose from. The low-end model, which is what I have been using for the past thirty-five years and still functions well, is a twenty-one quart enamel-coated steel canner with a wire rack that holds either 7 pint jars or 7 quart jars. The high-end model is basically the same pot, but it's made of stainless steel. You can get larger sizes that will hold more jars, but the concept is the same for all of them. Also on the market, though you may need to dig around a bit for it, is an electric canner. This is a self-heating unit that you plug in. Electric canners are much more expensive (hundreds of dollars versus tens of dollars), but one might be necessary depending upon the type of stovetop you have. Regardless of the size or type, your water-bath canner should have the following features:

❖ A lid to cover the pot. This keeps the heat inside so that the water stays at boiling temperatures during processing.

❖ A metal rack that keeps the jars off the bottom of the canner and helps keep them upright and separated during processing.

❖ Sides tall enough so that, when sitting on the rack, the jars can be covered with at least 1 to 2 inches of boiling water and an additional 1 to 2 inches of airspace (to keep the water from boiling over).

We're not talking about a big outlay of money here. As of this writing, there are a number of canners readily available for thirty to fifty dollars. There are also starter kits, which include the canner and special equipment that we'll mention shortly, for just a few dollars more than the cost of the canner. You will easily recoup your investment during your first season, and you'll have a canner that will serve you for many years.

PRESSURE CANNERS

Pressure canners (similar to pressure cookers, but larger and designed specifically for canning) are a bit more complex and require a bit more of a financial investment, but they are definitely something that you'll want to investigate once you get comfortable with water-bath canning. While a water-bath canner has a loose-fitting lid that keeps the heat in and helps maintain the boiling water temperature, pressure canners have tight-fitting lids with special vents and valves that allow carefully controlled pressure to build within the pot and then safely escape when the processing is over. The higher the pressure, the hotter the steam. The home pressure canners

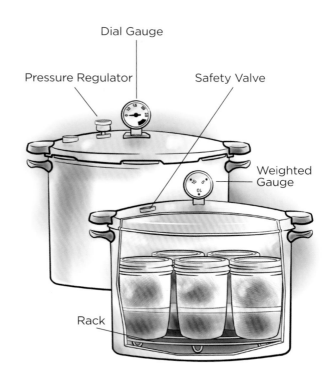

Pressure canners come in two basic styles: dial gauge and weighted gauge. If using an older model, be sure that all parts are in good working condition.

that we'll be working with use pressures in the range of 5, 10, and 15 pounds per square inch (psi) and can heat the steam to 240 degrees Fahrenheit. Each canner comes with its own specific directions for use. Read and follow those directions carefully. We'll discuss general procedures, but your manufacturer is the final authority.

There are two types of pressure canners, and they share many of the same features, including a lid that attaches securely to the base and possibly a gasket or a cover lock. On the lid, there is an open vent to let air and steam exhaust, a weight to close or restrict the vent and thus raise the steam pressure inside, and a safety valve or plug that will open if the inside pressure gets unsafe. There is a rack to keep the jars off the bottom of the pot and allow the steam to circulate around the jars. The pot must be deep enough to accommodate the desired jars without interfering with the lid closure. The main difference between pressure canners is the kind of gauge each uses to tell what the pressure is.

❖ **Dial-gauge pressure canners** have a dial with an arrow (like a clock face) that shows you exactly what the pressure is. These canners will have an opening for an air vent and a weight (called a *petcock*) that sits on the vent to maintain the pressure.

❖ **Weighted-gauge pressure canners** use a weight rather than a dial to regulate the pressure. There are a couple of different types: one is a small, circular disk (think undersized hockey puck). There are three holes on the outside rim, one each for 5, 10, and 15 pounds per square inch. Place the weight on the vent using the correct hole for the pressure stated in your recipe. The other type is a three-piece weight that you put on the vent. Add one, two, or three pieces (5, 10, or 15 pounds per square inch) to create the pressure called for in your recipe. With either type, when the steam starts to escape through the vent, it makes the weighted gauge move and make noise (you will hear the steam hissing, and see the gauge jiggling or rocking). You'll know that you've reached the correct pressure when this happens a few times per minute.

In choosing the type, it's really a matter of personal preference. Generally, the weighted-gauge pressure canners tend to be less expensive than the dial-gauge ones. And the dial-gauge canners must be checked for accuracy each year, as they can lose accurate calibration. Check with your manufacturer or your local Cooperative Extension Service for information about calibrating dial gauges. Though you can easily spend more, you should be able to find either type for around a hundred dollars.

CANNER SAFETY CHECK

Once you have your canner, regardless of style, check it annually to make sure it is in good working order and free from dents and dings. Examine gaskets, gauges, racks, vents, and dials to be sure they are free from residue or obstruction and show no warpage. For pressure canners, check that the lid fits securely.

JARS, LIDS, AND BANDS

Regardless of what your mother or grandmother used when they canned (I've got two-piece, bail-topped jars, zinc and ceramic screw lids, and other pieces of memorabilia from my mother's kitchen), the only safe and approved container for home canning is a special glass canning jar, known as a "Mason jar" in memory of American tinsmith John L. Mason, who invented the jar in 1858. Along with the jar is a two-piece metal closure composed of a threaded metal screw band and a flat, round, single-use, specially coated lid whose underside has a channel of food-safe sealing compound. When put together, the

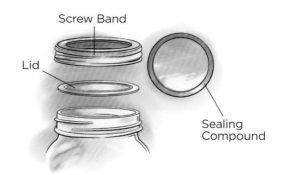

Screw Band

Lid

Sealing Compound

lid fits neatly on the jar with the sealing compound next to the glass rim and is held in place by the screw band.

What could be more iconic of home food preservation than the glass Mason jar! The qualities embodied in these jars account for half of the appeal of canning. They come in a variety of sizes and shapes, tailored perfectly to the proposed contents. They are clear glass, which is a perfect environment for storing foods because they can be easily sterilized in boiling water, and they show off their contents. The jars also won't absorb odors, flavors, or colors, and they are almost indefinitely reusable as well as recyclable.

When selecting jars for your canning needs, there are several things to consider:

Using two-piece screw bands and lids is the easiest way to seal your canned goods. These are readily available during canning season. Remember, you can reuse the bands, but the lids are single-use only.

❖ **Style.** The main style difference between jars is the width of the mouth (the opening at the top). The most widely used jars are called "regular" mouth and have a 2⅝-inch diameter opening at the top. These are suitable for most canning recipes, from beans and corn to tomatoes and relish. Another alternative is a "wide-mouth" jar, which is just that. The top opening is 3⅛ inches in diameter and allows you to easily insert larger fruit sections, such as peach halves or whole pickles. Both regular and wide-mouth jars have a distinctive narrowing, or neck, below the top. A third style of jar is known as a "jelly" jar. They generally come in smaller sizes, often have decorative designs pressed into the glass, and don't have a neck. Now that canning is becoming so fashionable, you can also find a number of boutique jars that are lovely for gift giving. I keep a supply of regular-mouth pints and quarts for the foods that I can for my family, and a variety of 4- and 8-ounce jelly jars for jams and relishes.

❖ **Size.** Jars range in size from half-cup jelly jars to half-gallon juice jars. Factors to consider include your family size, the serving size, and/or your intended use for the jar. For example, if you are making jam as a gift, you may want to use half-cup jelly jars so that you can make more gifts, but if you are making it for your family's use, then the pint jar is probably fine and will make less work for you.

Jelly jars (left) are usually 8 ounces and have straight sides. Standard pint and quart jars have curved necks.

❖ **Quality.** Make sure that the jars that you select are intended for home canning. True canning jars have a threaded neck designed to engage with canning bands. The jar must have a smooth, flat top that is free from chips so that the lid forms a tight seal. It's tempting to want to reuse old mayonnaise jars or other products whose jar openings have the same diameter as regular Mason jars, but *do not use them!* They are intended for one-time use and may crack during processing. Also beware of picking up used jars in a tag sale. If you are careful and can check each jar carefully, you might get a good bargain. But you might also get jars that have chips or cracks, or jars that are not of authentic canning quality.

Once you choose the style of your jar, your choice of lid and band is made for you. You'll use a regular-size lid and band for a regular-mouth jar, regardless of the jar's capacity. The same is true for wide-mouth jars. When purchasing jars, especially if you are buying a known brand such as Ball or Kerr, the package comes with lids and bands. The lids are for one-time use only, but you can reuse the bands for years, until they get too rusty to close smoothly.

One last thought about Mason jars and bargain hunting: Bear in mind that the jars that you invest in for your family's use are just that—an investment. As of this writing, a dozen name-brand quart Mason jars with lids and bands costs less than ten dollars at full price. If you plan to can a lot, that initial investment can be substantial. But when you consider that this is a one-time investment, the cost is much more palatable. Even with the jelly jars (which are similar in cost to regular Mason jars, even though they are smaller in size) that you plan to give away, the cost is very modest when compared with other gift options.

MASON JAR WARNING

Mason jars are designed to withstand the heat of boiling water and pressure canners, but they are not designed to withstand quick changes in temperature, like a Pyrex dish might. Don't use them in the oven, and always make sure that they are hot or warm before you fill them with boiling foods and liquids, or else they might crack.

UTENSILS

The utensils needed for canning are pretty simple and inexpensive, but for the most part, they are indispensable! These little gadgets are to canning what fire or the wheel must have been to prehistoric people—life-changing improvements. They'll set you back maybe twenty bucks but will last a lifetime. Some manufacturers put together a kit of all of the utensils, which is probably the smartest way to go.

❖ **Jar lifters** are specially designed "claws" that clamp down around the neck of the jar and hold it snugly while you lift it in and out of the boiling water or pressure canner. They work on compression, as my husband the engineer would explain. The tighter you squeeze the handles together, the tighter the curved, rubber-coated tongs grab the jar neck. *Do not use regular kitchen tongs!* They might work, but they won't give you that secure hold

Don't try to lift your jars in or out of your canner without a jar lifter that is specially designed for canning. The safety that they offer is well worth the couple of dollars that they cost.

that you need as you pull a jar of boiling fruit out of a pot of boiling water. If the tongs release, you risk losing all your hard work and possibly getting a serious burn.

Look for a canning funnel that is made of plastic or stainless steel, and steer clear of Grandma's old aluminum one.

❖ **Canning funnels** are similar to regular kitchen funnels except that they are specially designed to fit into a standard-size canning jar and have a spacious opening to make filling your jars easy and dripless. As you'll learn shortly, this is very import to ensure a perfect seal. Look for either BPA-free plastic or stainless steel funnels. Avoid aluminum because you may be working with high-acid foods, and acid reacts with aluminum to form aluminum salts, which may be a health risk.

Lid lifters are more than just "nice-to-haves." They help prevent burned fingers and keep the sterile lids from being contaminated.

❖ **Lid lifters** or **magnetic wands** are essentially plastic sticks with magnets at the end. They allow you to lift the metal lid from the boiling water that sterilizes it and place it on the top of the jar—no burned fingers, no germs on the lids.

❖ **Bubble probes** are narrow, nonmetallic tools about the length of a quart jar. A thin kitchen spatula will work just fine, too. Use one of these tools to help trapped air bubbles escape from inside the jars after you have filled them.

❖ **Headspace tools** come in different packages. Some canning funnels have markings to show headspace. One manufacturer has a combination bubble probe and headspace tool—very handy to ensure that you are allowing the necessary headspace (the distance between the top of the jar and the level of the filled contents). A standard ruler is just as helpful.

❖ **Jelly bags or cheesecloth** are handy if you plan to make and can juices. These allow you to easily separate the juice from the pulp. You'll hear more about these in chapter 5, "Jams, Jellies, and More."

❖ **The usual kitchen implements** also come in handy when canning. In addition to these canning specialty items,

Cheesecloth is a versatile tool to have in your canning kitchen. For clearer juices and jelly, use several layers of cheesecloth when straining the pulp.

you'll need the following items typically found in most kitchens: cutting board, colander, blanching pot with basket, ladles, large slotted spoons, bowls, clean cloths and towels, hot pads, timer or clock, measuring cups and spoons, and sharp knives. There are other nice-to-have items that are useful in certain situations, but we'll mention those with the specific recipes. No reason to get unnecessary equipment!

WHERE TO GET THIS STUFF

Depending upon where you live and what season it is, you can often find a nice supply of canning and preserving products at your local grocery, hardware, or warehouse store. You might have to ask someone, as sometimes the jars and canners are squirreled away in a corner because the stock person didn't know what they were. Should you have any trouble finding canning equipment locally, there are numerous online resources. See Resources, or simply search the Internet for "canning supplies" and you will be gratified with a long list of links. I've had good success with the site www.freshpreserving.com. It's run by Jarden Home Products, the company that owns canning giants Ball and Kerr. The site offers a great deal of information; free, tested recipes; and quality canning products that are reasonably priced. Equally helpful is a site called Kitchen Krafts (www.kitchenkrafts.com).

If you have no canning equipment, I highly recommend purchasing a basic canning starter kit. For the cost of just the water-bath canner alone, you can get the canner and all the nifty tools to go with it and a starter supply of jars, lids, and bands.

HOT PACK VERSUS RAW PACK

One of the decisions you have to make when canning is whether to pack cooked or raw food into the canning jar. Generally, the recipe that you use will tell you the preferred method for that particular recipe.

❖ *Raw packing* (also called cold packing) means packing uncooked food into your warm jars, and then covering it with boiling water to the correct headspace level. Be sure to pack produce tightly (but don't crush it) because it will shrink during processing.

❖ *Hot packing* means boiling or cooking (according to the recipe) your food first in water, syrup, or brine, and then packing the hot food and hot liquid into the jar. Many people prefer this method—even though it involves an extra step—because the cooked fruits and vegetables are softer and more pliable, enabling you to fill your jars fuller and use fewer jars. Some folks feel that hot-packed fruits and vegetables have better color and flavor, especially when water-bath canned. Remember, however, that because there won't be shrinkage, you don't want to over-pack the jars.

When you hot-pack foods for water-bath canning, you'll see that often the processing time is reduced because the foods are already hot and at least partially cooked. With pressure canning, there will be no difference in the processing time because the heat required to bring up the necessary pressure will cook the food in the jars. As you'll see, you'll start counting the processing time only when the canner has reached the correct temperature or pressure.

THE CANNING PROCESS OVERVIEW

While the differences between water-bath canning and pressure canning are significant in terms of food safety and investment in equipment, the actual steps are very similar.

1. Prepare your workspace. An important part of that preparation is making sure that everything is as clean as you can make it. You don't need to sterilize your kitchen, but you need to eliminate as many microorganisms as possible.

2. Gather and thoroughly clean your canning utensils (funnel, jar and lid lifters, bubble probe, headspace measure). Depending on what you are canning, this will also include such items as the cutting board, colander, blanching basket, food mill or strainer, ladles, large slotted spoons, bowls, clean cloths and towels, hot pads, timer or clock, and sharp knives.

3. Check your canner and make sure that all parts are in good working order.

4. For water-bath canners, add hot water to a level that will cover the jars, and start to heat. The water should be simmering (not boiling) when you place the jars in the bath.

5. Prepare your jars, bands, and lids (see the sidebar).

6. Decide whether to hot-pack or cold-pack (raw-pack) the food.

7. For fruit only: if syrup-packing, make your syrup and keep it at a low simmer. See the sidebar "Sugar Syrups" on page 87 for types of sugar syrups and how to make them.

PREPARING JARS, LIDS, AND BANDS

Whether your jars are new or used, follow these steps to prepare them for canning:

1. Check each jar carefully for chips or cracks. Run your finger around the top edge to make sure it is perfectly smooth. Even a little chip can prevent proper sealing and cause the food to spoil.

2. Select the correct size of band for the jars that you are using. Bands should be clean and free from rust, but they do not need to be sterilized.

3. Wash jars carefully in hot, soapy water and rinse thoroughly. The easiest method is to wash in an automatic dishwasher using the hottest setting, and then leave

8. Work in canner-load quantities (the amount that you'll need to fill one canner load—usually that's seven jars—to ensure the highest quality). See the appendix for approximate conversions.

9. Examine and wash your produce carefully, changing the water frequently. Prepare the produce as described in your recipe (remove stems, seeds, and pits, and cut as desired.)

10. Treat produce to prevent darkening, if necessary, following the instructions in "Treating for Discoloration" in the appendix. This is generally only for light-colored fruits such as apples, peaches, apricots, nectarines, and pears.

11. If in the recipe, blanch the produce to remove any skins. (See "All about Blanching" in the appendix.)

12. If hot-packing, heat or cook the produce according to the recipe. Keep both the produce and the liquid warm.

These tomatoes have been blanched, their skins peeled, and quartered, so they're ready to go. You can can them as-is or turn them into a hearty tomato sauce.

the jars in the warm dishwasher until they are ready to fill, removing only one warm jar at a time. If you don't have a dishwasher, keep your clean jars warm by covering them in warm water and simmering at 180 degrees Fahrenheit until you are ready to use them. *Do not fill cold jars with hot food—the glass is likely to crack!*

Select the correct size lid for the jars that you are using. Use only new lids so that the seal is fresh. Place lids in a pan of water and simmer at 180 degrees Fahrenheit for ten minutes before using. Do not boil them, as this can affect the sealing compound. Leave the lids in the warm water, removing them one at a time, as needed, using a lid lifter.

Hold the jar upright when lifting it in and out of the canner.

13. Working with one jar at a time, fill each jar to the level stated in the recipe—no partially full jars.

14. Using the jar lifter, grab the filled jar below the neck and place it carefully into the canner (keeping it upright). Don't worry; the water will not leak into the jars. Repeat with the other jars until you fill the canner.

15. Process the finished jars for the time required using the method called for in the recipe, adjusting as necessary for altitude. See "Altitude Adjustment" in the appendix.

16. Using the jar lifter, remove the processed jars from the canner, keeping the jars upright as you lift them. Don't worry if a little water puddles on the lids; it will soon evaporate. Place the jars on a dry towel in a draft-free location to cool completely. Leave a few inches between each jar to allow the air to circulate. The bands will likely be loose, but do not tighten them! That could disturb the seal. It will take from twelve to twenty-four hours for the jars to cool.

17. Soon, you will hear a gratifying sound: *ping*! As the contents cool, they contract and form a vacuum, which pulls the lid down tightly to form a seal, making a sound as the lid goes from *convex* (curved upward) to *concave* (curved downward). Do not push down on the lids until the jars are completely cool.

18. When the jars are completely cool (within twelve to twenty-four hours), test the seals. Look at each lid. If it's concave, that's good. Then tap the lid; it should make a high *ping* sound, not a dull *tap*. Not all lids will sound exactly the same (these aren't highly tuned musical instruments you're dealing with). Lastly, remove the band and gently push up on the lid. It should not budge. If it does, the jar is not sealed. You can process it again following the same directions (use a clean jar and a new, heated lid) or store it in the refrigerator and use it soon.

19. If the lids sealed properly, label and store your newly canned produce, and remember to use it within a year.

As the jars cool, you're likely to hear the gratifying *ping* that tells you the lid is sealing. When tapping the cooled lids, the sound will be high-pitched, not dull.

Filling the Jars

Finally, the fun part! You've done all the preparation, now you get the gratification of seeing vegetables and fruits fill up your jars. While you're having fun, be sure to follow these steps carefully and exactly.

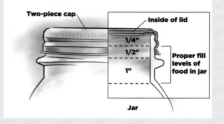

Remember this little illustration from chapter 3? Don't forget to leave the correct headspace when filling jars!

1. Take one hot jar from the dishwasher or warm water (empty water, if necessary).

2. Put the jar on a flat towel on the countertop.

3. Place the canning funnel into the top of the jar.

4. Pack food into the jar, allowing for sufficient headspace.

   • If cold-packing (or raw-packing), add boiling liquid to just cover the food. The top of the liquid should be at the headspace mark.

   • If hot-packing, press the food down. Depending upon how firm or soft your food is, the liquid may automatically cover the food. If not, add extra liquid as needed to just cover the food and reach the specified headspace.

5. Remove any air bubbles (visible or hidden) that may be trapped around the food by inserting the bubble probe (or nonmetallic spatula) gently down the sides of the jar and pressing or jiggling the food to force the air out. You'll see any bubbles rise to the top. Repeat in several places to ensure that all the bubbles have escaped. If necessary, add more liquid so that you have the correct headspace. The jars must be full; you can't can a half-full jar.

6. Remove the funnel and wipe the rim of the jar using a clean, damp cloth to remove any pieces of food, syrup, or brine that may have landed on the rim. *If you don't have a perfectly clean rim, the lid will not seal properly.*

7. Using the lid-lifter wand, pick up one lid, attaching the magnet from the wand to the outside of the lid (the side with writing that does not have the sealing compound).

8. Place the lid onto the rim of the jar. Place you finger in the center of the lid to hold it in place as you remove the magnetic wand.

9. Holding the lid in place, screw on the metal band to "fingertip tightness." That means not too tight but not too loose. Just screw it on so that it's closed snugly; don't force it. As the jars process, any captured air needs to be able to escape. When reading common canning recipes or instructions, this is referred to as "adjusting the lids."

Busy day in the kitchen! When placing the jars to cool, leave a little space between them, but don't put them near a drafty door.

WATER-BATH CANNING

We've covered the basic steps for water-bath canning and pressure canning. Here are a few specifics for water-bath canning and recipes for common fruits and tomato products.

PROCESS OVERVIEW

1. Put the rack in the bottom of canner and fill the canner about half full of hot water. Start to heat the water before you fill your jars so that it reaches a simmer (180 degrees Fahrenheit) by the time you are ready to put your filled jars in. Depending upon the number and size of the jars, you may need to add boiling water so that the jars are all covered with 1 to 2 inches of water. Don't pour the water directly onto the jars.

2. Put the cover on the canner, turn the temperature on high, and bring the water to a full boil. Start timing according to recipe. Keep the canner covered and the water boiling the entire time. You can tweak the temperature setting a bit, as long as you maintain a full boil for the entire canning time. Add more boiling water, if needed, to keep the water level above the jars.

3. When the jars have been boiled for the recommended amount of time, turn off the heat and remove the canner lid. Wait five minutes before removing the jars.

Start timing the processing time when the water comes to a full boil.

Sugar Syrups

It's time for a refresher course in sugar syrups—you're going to need it for many of the following recipes. When preparing syrup packs for either canning or freezing, use the proportions below. You may use honey for part of the syrup, though it will influence the flavor of the fruit. To prepare the syrup, combine the ingredients in a pan and bring the mixture to a boil. Simmer until the sugar is completely dissolved. You will need approximately ½ to ¾ cups of syrup for each pint and 1 to 1½ cups for each quart that you can.

TYPE OF SYRUP	PERCENTAGE OF SUGAR	CUPS OF SUGAR	CUPS OF HONEY	CUPS OF WATER	YIELD IN CUPS OF SYRUP
Extra-light	20	1½	0	5½	6
Light	30	2¼	0	5¼	6½
Medium	40	3¼	0	5	7
Heavy	50	4¼	0	4¼	7
Honey	0	1	1	4	5

ABOUT THE RECIPES

High-acid foods are the *only* foods that can be canned by using the water-bath canning process. For some of these high-acid foods, you can also use pressure canning, if you like, but *the reverse is not true: low-acid foods can only be processed using a pressure canner.* Canning guidelines for low-acid foods are provided in the next section.

The following are recipes for canning some of your favorite fruits and tomatoes. These recipes have been tested and approved by the USDA. Follow the instructions exactly—especially the length of time for processing. Raw-pack products generally require longer processing times than hot-pack products. These times apply to locations between sea level and 1,000 feet. If you live at an altitude higher than that, adjust the processing time according to the figures in "Altitude Adjustment" in the appendix. If you want to consider pressure-canning any of these high-acid foods (this is especially beneficial for tomatoes), see the chart on page 195 in the appendix.

Many of the recipes are intentionally flexible so that you can tailor the recipe to the amount of produce you have. These will tell you about how much produce you need for a canned pint or quart; then you can adjust accordingly.

Water-Bath Canning Recipes

For all recipes, after filling jars to the required headspace, remove any bubbles; wipe the rims clean; adjust the lids; and process the finished jars for the stated time, adjusting as necessary for altitude (see "Altitude Adjustment" in the appendix).

Ava's Applesauce

This recipe is perfect for children because you don't need to add any sugar. Just ask my granddaughter Ava! It's super easy, too, because you don't need to peel and core the apples.

Yield: Flexible

Ingredients:

❖ Apples, 2½ to 3½ pounds per quart (McIntosh, Gala, Paula Red, Jonathan, or Golden Delicious are good choices)

❖ Ascorbic acid

❖ Water

Special equipment: Food mill (preferred) or food strainer

1. Wash the apples thoroughly, cutting out any bad spots. Really clean the blossom end.

2. Cut the apple into 6 slices—don't worry about removing the seeds or skin.

3. Treat the apples for darkening using the ascorbic acid (see "Treating for Discoloration" in the appendix).

4. Place the apples, dripping wet, into a very heavy saucepan. This is key: the pan needs to have a thick aluminum core so that the apples don't scorch. A flimsy saucepan can work, but you'll need to keep the temperature very low to prevent burning.

5. Fill the heavy pot nearly to the top with the cut apples. Add a little bit of water. For a 3-quart pot, I add about ¼ cup of water.

6. Turn the stovetop temperature to medium high (or medium if you don't have a heavy-duty pot) and cook the apples until they are very soft and the peel falls off the flesh. Check on them now and then, stirring occasionally. Depending upon the pot size and heat, this will be about 20 minutes. (I do multiple pots at one time.)

7. While the apples are cooking get your jars, lids, and other canning equipment ready so that you can put the sauce into the jars without having to reheat too much.

8. When finished cooking, press the cooked apples through a food strainer or food mill to remove the sauce from the skins, stems, and seeds. If you have a fancy mixer, there are attachments that you can buy to do this, but I've used a crank-style food mill for years, and it works great. It's amazing how much sauce you can get this way. Your yield will be much greater than for recipes that call for peeled and cored apples.

9. As you finish each strainerful, empty the sauce into a large pot to keep warm until you have finished cooking and straining all of the apples.

10. Heat the sauce to boiling, being careful not to scorch.

11. Working one jar at a time, pour the boiling sauce into the jar, leaving a $\frac{1}{2}$-inch headspace.

12. Process the finished jars in a water-bath canner: 15 minutes for pints and 20 minutes for quarts.

WHAT'S A FOOD MILL?

You might not find a food mill in every kitchen, but it's a "must have" for making applesauce, tomato juice, and other strained foods. You can easily find them in most housewares departments, many hardware stores, and specialty kitchen shops. While you can pay more, a basic model will run you about thirty dollars.

Apple Juice

Yield: 6 quarts

Ingredients:

- 24 pounds apples
- 2 quarts water

1. Wash and drain the apples. Remove their blossom and stem ends, then chop and place the apples in a large, heavyweight pot.

2. Add water, and cook until tender, stirring occasionally. Strain the cooked apples through a jelly bag or layered cheesecloth to separate the pulp from the juice (see "The Art of the Jelly Bag" in the appendix.)

3. Heat the juice for 5 minutes until it reaches 190°F. Do not boil.

4. Ladle hot juice into hot jars, leaving a 1/4-inch headspace.

5. Process the finished jars: 10 minutes, regardless of size.

Apple Rings

Yield: 6 pints or 3 quarts

Ingredients:

- 10 pounds firm apples, (Macoun and Winesap are good; avoid McIntosh and Cortland)
- Ascorbic acid
- 4 cups sugar
- 4 cups water
- Red food color (optional)
- Cinnamon stick (optional)

1. Wash and core but do not peel the apples. Slice them into 1/4-inch rings; treat them with ascorbic acid to prevent darkening according to "Treating for Discoloration" in the appendix; and drain them.

2. Make syrup by combining sugar, water, coloring, and cinnamon, and boil the mixture for 5 minutes. Add the apples; then reduce the heat and simmer for 35 minutes.

3. Remove the rings from the syrup and allow them to cool. Return the syrup to a boil.

4. Pack the rings loosely in hot jars, and ladle hot syrup over the rings, leaving 1/2-inch headspace. Discard the cinnamon stick.

5. Process the finished jars: 15 minutes for pints or 20 minutes for quarts.

Berries—Whole

This recipe is for blackberries, black and red raspberries, blueberries, and currants. Freezing works better for strawberries. Use raw packing for very soft berries, such as red raspberries, and use hot packing for firmer berries. Select firm, ripe, perfect fruit, and remove any caps and stems.

Yield: Flexible

Ingredients:

❖ Fruit, about 3 pounds per quart

❖ Light to medium syrup

To raw-pack: Make a light to medium syrup according to "Sugar Syrups" on page 87 and keep it hot. Wash and drain the berries. Fill the jars with berries, leaving $\frac{1}{2}$-inch headspace; gently shake the jar to settle the berries. Ladle hot syrup over the berries, leaving the same $\frac{1}{2}$-inch headspace. Process the finished jars: 15 minutes for pints and 20 minutes for quarts.

To hot-pack: Wash, drain, and measure the berries; place them in the pot. Add $\frac{1}{4}$ to $\frac{1}{2}$ cup sugar per quart (to taste); let stand in a cool place for 2 hours. Cook the berries and sugar slowly until the sugar is dissolved, the berries are heated through, and a sugar syrup forms. Ladle the hot syrup and berries into the jars, leaving a $\frac{1}{2}$-inch headspace. If you don't have enough syrup to cover to the same $\frac{1}{2}$-inch headspace, add boiling water. Process the finished jars: 15 minutes for both pints and quarts.

Brandied Pears

Yield: 8 pints or 4 quarts

Ingredients:

❖ 10 pounds pears

❖ Ascorbic acid

❖ 6 cups sugar

❖ 4 cups water

❖ 3 cups white brandy (for clear syrup) or other brandy, as preferred

1. Wash, peel, core, and halve the pears. Treat them with ascorbic acid to prevent darkening according to the instructions in "Treating for Discoloration" in the appendix, and let them sit in the liquid while making the syrup.

2. Make the syrup by combining the sugar and water in a large pot; bring this to a boil.

3. Drain the pears and add them to the syrup to create a single layer of pears on the bottom of the pot; cook for about 5 minutes or until just tender. Do not undercook or the fruit will darken. Remove the pears and place them in a deep bowl. Repeat with additional layers if necessary, until all pears have cooked in the syrup. Set pears aside.

4. Boil the syrup (without the pears) for about 15 minutes or until thickened. Remove from heat, and add the brandy.

5. Pack the pears into hot jars, leaving a ½-inch headspace. Ladle hot syrup over the pears, leaving ¼-inch headspace.

6. Process the finished jars: 15 minutes for both pints and quarts.

Cherries

Select bright, mature, uniformly colored eating or cooking cherries. Wash them, remove the stems, and drain well. Cherries can be pitted or not. If pitted, treat with ascorbic acid to prevent darkening according to the instructions in "Treating for Discoloration" in the appendix. If not pitted, prick each end with a clean, pointed object to prevent bursting during processing.

Yield: 4 pints or 2 quarts

Ingredients:

❖ 5 pounds cherries

❖ Ascorbic acid (if cherries are pitted)

❖ Light, medium, or heavy syrup, depending on cherry type

❖ Apple or white-grape juice, if desired, for hot packing

To raw-pack: Make light or medium syrup for sweet cherries or medium to heavy syrup for tart cherries according to "Sugar Syrups" on page 87; keep hot. Place the cherries in jars, shaking gently to settle them and leaving ½-inch headspace. Ladle hot syrup over the cherries, leaving the same ½-inch headspace. Process the finished jars: 25 minutes for both pints and quarts.

To hot-pack: Place cherries in a large saucepan; add a ½ cup water, juice, or syrup (see above) per quart of cherries. Bring to a boil. Pack the cherries in hot jars, leaving a ½-inch headspace. Fill the jars with hot liquid, leaving a ½-inch headspace. Process the finished jars: 15 minutes for pints and 20 minutes for quarts.

Grape Juice

Select sweet, deep-colored, mature, firm fruit. Concord grapes work well.

Yield: Flexible

Ingredients:

- Grapes, 3½ pounds grapes per quart of juice
- 1 cup water per gallon crushed grapes
- 1–2 cups sugar per gallon crushed grapes

1. Wash, stem, and drain the grapes. Crush and measure them to determine how much you have, then place them in a large saucepan.

2. Add water and heat to 190°F; do not boil. Strain juice through a damp jelly bag or several layers of damp cheesecloth (see "The Art of the Jelly Bag" in the appendix). Refrigerate the juice for 24 to 48 hours to allow sediment and tartaric acid to settle.

3. Ladle juice from the pan into another container, being careful not to stir or disturb the sediment. Strain the juice again, and then measure it.

4. Add sugar to taste.

5. Reheat and stir the juice until the sugar is dissolved and the juice just begins to boil. Fill the hot jars immediately to a ¼-inch headspace.

6. Process the finished jars: 5 minutes for both pints and quarts, 10 minutes for half-gallons.

Peaches, Nectarines, and Apricots

Choose mature, ripe fruit—the ideal quality for eating or cooking. For the best results, I recommend the hot-packing method on this one.

Yield: Flexible

Ingredients:

- Desired fruit, 2½ pounds per quart
- Ascorbic acid
- Light to medium syrup
- Apple or white-grape juice (optional)
- Water (optional)

1. Wash the fruit thoroughly. (For peaches only: blanch them in boiling water for 30 to 60 seconds, cool them, and slip off the skins [see "All About Blanching" in the appendix].) Cut the fruit in half, remove the pits, and slice if desired.

2. Prepare a very light to medium syrup as desired according to "Sugar Syrups" on page 87, or use fruit juice or water. Add the manufacturer-recommended amount of ascorbic acid, and bring the syrup or juice to a boil.

3. Place the fruit in a large saucepan with the preferred liquid and bring to a boil. Fill each jar with fruit (cut-side down) and hot liquid to a 1/2-inch headspace.

4. Process the finished jars: 20 minutes for pints and 25 minutes for quarts.

Pears

Choose mature, ripe fruit that would be ideal quality for eating or cooking.

Yield: Flexible

Ingredients:

- Pears, 2 1/2 pounds per quart
- Ascorbic acid
- Very light to medium syrup
- Apple or white grape juice (optional)
- Water (optional)

1. Wash and peel the pears; cut them lengthwise; and remove the cores using a melon baller. Treat the fruit with ascorbic acid to prevent darkening, and keep it in the solution while preparing the syrup.

2. Prepare a very light to medium syrup according to "Sugar Syrups" on page 87, or use fruit juice or water instead, and bring to a boil.

3. Drain the pears; place them in a large saucepan with the syrup or juice and bring everything to a boil. Turn off heat. Fill each jar with the fruit and liquid to a 1/2-inch headspace.

4. Process the finished jars: 20 minutes for pints and 25 minutes for quarts.

Plums

I highly recommend Green Gage plums. These are very sweet and flavorful, great for eating, baking, and preserving.

Yield: Flexible

Ingredients:

❖ Plums, 2 pounds of fruit per quart

❖ Very light to medium syrup

❖ Water (optional)

1. Wash and stem the plums. If canning whole, prick the skin on two sides. If you prefer, cut the plums in half and pit them.

2. If using syrup, prepare very light to medium syrup. If using water, bring it to a boil.

3. **To hot-pack:** Place the plums in a saucepan to create a single layer of fruit on the bottom of the pan and cover with hot syrup or water; boil for 2 minutes. Remove the plums and keep them hot. Continue until all plums are cooked. When finished with the plums, remove the cooking liquid from the heat; add all the plums back in; cover the pan; and let stand 20 to 30 minutes. Pack the hot plums into hot jars to a 1/2-inch headspace. Return the cooking liquid to a simmer; ladle hot liquid over the plums to the same 1/2-inch headspace. **To raw-pack:** pack plums firmly into hot jars to a 1/2-inch headspace; ladle hot syrup to the same 1/2-inch headspace.

3. Process the finished jars: 20 minutes for pints and 25 minutes for quarts.

Water-Bath Canning Tomato Recipes

Following are a number of tomato recipes. Canning is an easy and economical way to use the bounty of tomatoes from your garden. For all tomato recipes:

❖ Select only disease-free, firm, vine-ripened fruit. Do not can tomatoes from dead or frost-killed vines.

❖ The acid level of tomatoes can be inconsistent. The riper the tomato, the lower the acid level. Green tomatoes are higher in acidity than ripe ones and may be added to any of these recipes. Some newer varieties, such as yellow tomatoes, have lower acid levels. To ensure safe acidity levels in whole, crushed, or juiced tomatoes, add 2 tablespoons bottled lemon juice (or ½ teaspoon citric acid) to each quart of tomatoes. Halve that amount for pints. Add the juice or acid before you fill the jars. If desired, add a teaspoon or two of sugar to offset the acid taste.

❖ If you want to pressure-can tomatoes—some people feel it results in a better product— see "Pressure-Canning Processing Times" in the appendix.

❖ As with all recipes, after filling the jars to the required headspace, remove any bubbles; wipe the rims clean; adjust the lids; and process for the stated amount of time. Where salt is indicated, use canning salt.

Tomatoes—Whole or Halved

Yield: Flexible

Ingredients:

❖ Tomatoes, 3 pounds per quart

❖ Water

- 2 tablespoons lemon juice or ¼ teaspoon citric acid per quart
- 1 teaspoon salt per quart or ½ teaspoon salt per pint (optional)
- 1–2 teaspoons sugar to taste (optional)

1. Wash the tomatoes. Blanch them in boiling water for 30 to 60 seconds or until the skins split; immerse them in cold water; and slip off the skins (see "All About Blanching" in the appendix). Cut out the cores and any bruised or discolored spots. Leave the tomatoes whole or cut them in half.

2. Add your preferred acid to the hot jars. Add salt and sugar, if desired.

3. **To raw-pack:** Boil water. Fill jars with raw tomatoes to a ½-inch headspace; then ladle hot water over the raw tomatoes, also to a ½-inch headspace. **To hot-pack:** Place the tomatoes in a large saucepan, add water to cover, and boil gently for 5 minutes. Fill the jars with hot tomatoes and hot cooking liquid to a ½-inch headspace.

4. Process the finished jars: 40 minutes for pints and 45 minutes for quarts.

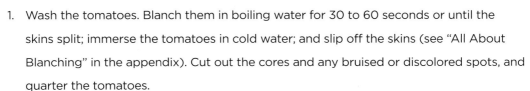

Tomatoes—Crushed and Packed in Own Juice

Yield: Flexible

Ingredients:

- Tomatoes, 3¾ pounds per quart
- 2 tablespoons lemon juice or ¼ teaspoon citric acid per quart
- 1 teaspoon salt per quart or ½ teaspoon salt per pint (optional)
- 1–2 teaspoons sugar to taste (optional)

1. Wash the tomatoes. Blanch them in boiling water for 30 to 60 seconds or until the skins split; immerse the tomatoes in cold water; and slip off the skins (see "All About Blanching" in the appendix). Cut out the cores and any bruised or discolored spots, and quarter the tomatoes.

2. Place a layer of quartered tomatoes in a large saucepan; heat while crushing to extract juice. Bring the tomatoes and juice to a boil; gradually add the remaining quartered tomatoes, stirring constantly. Crushing the remaining tomatoes is optional.

3. After all tomatoes have been added, boil gently for 5 minutes. The tomatoes will be soft.

4. Add lemon juice or citric acid to the hot jars. Add salt and sugar, if desired.

5. Ladle the hot tomatoes and juice into hot jars, leaving a ½-inch headspace.

6. Process the finished jars: 35 minutes for pints, and 45 minutes for quarts.

Tomato Juice

Yield: Flexible

Ingredients:

- Tomatoes, 3¼ pounds per quart
- 2 tablespoons lemon juice or ¼ teaspoon citric acid per quart
- 1 teaspoon salt per quart or ½ teaspoon salt per pint (optional)

1. Wash the tomatoes thoroughly; remove the stem and blossom ends along with any bruised or discolored portions. Quarter and place the tomatoes in a large saucepan. Simmer until soft, stirring occasionally to prevent sticking.

2. Remove cooked tomatoes from the heat and press them through a food mill or sieve to remove the skins and seeds.

3. Add 2 tablespoons lemon juice or ¼ teaspoon citric acid per quart.

4. Bring the juice to a boil; add salt if desired. Ladle hot juice into hot jars, leaving a ½-inch headspace.

5. Process the finished jars: 35 minutes for pints and 40 minutes for quarts.

Tomato Sauce (Unseasoned)

Yield: Flexible

Ingredients:

- Tomatoes, 6½ pounds per quart
- 2 tablespoons lemon juice or ¼ teaspoon citric acid per quart
- 1 teaspoon salt per quart or ½ teaspoon salt per pint (optional)
- 1–2 teaspoons sugar to taste (optional)

1. Follow the directions in the tomato juice recipe, above, but simmer the juice in a large-diameter, stainless or enamel-clad saucepan before ladling it into jars. Boil it slowly, stirring occasionally, until the sauce reaches the desired consistency. For thin sauce, reduce the volume by one-third; for thick sauce, reduce it by one-half.

2. Add 2 tablespoons lemon juice or ¼ teaspoon citric acid per quart to hot jars; add salt and sugar, if desired.

3. Ladle hot sauce into hot jars, leaving a ¼-inch headspace.

4. Process the finished jars: 35 minutes for pints and 40 minutes for quarts.

Tomato Sauce (Seasoned)

Yield: 5 pints

Ingredients:

- 20 pounds tomatoes
- 4 large onions, finely chopped
- 6 cloves garlic, finely chopped
- 1 tablespoon oregano
- 3 bay leaves
- 2 teaspoons salt
- 2 teaspoons fresh ground black pepper
- 1 teaspoon crushed red pepper (optional)
- 1 tablespoon sugar
- 2 tablespoons lemon juice or $\frac{1}{4}$ teaspoon citric acid per quart

1. Wash the tomatoes. Blanch them in boiling water for 30 to 60 seconds or until the skins split; immerse them in cold water; and slip off the skins (see "All About Blanching" in the appendix). Cut out the cores and any bruised or discolored spots, chop, and place in a large saucepan.
2. Add all other ingredients (except the acid). Bring the mixture to a boil and then simmer it for about 2 hours.
3. Press the sauce through a food mill or sieve; continue to cook the sauce until the volume is reduced by half or you reach your desired consistency.
4. Add 2 tablespoons lemon juice or $\frac{1}{4}$ teaspoon citric acid per quart to hot jars.
5. Ladle hot sauce into hot jars, leaving a $\frac{1}{2}$-inch headspace.
6. Process the finished jars: 35 minutes for both pints and half-pints.

PRESSURE CANNING

We covered the basic steps for both water-bath canning and pressure canning. Always read and follow the manufacturer's instructions for using your pressure canner, as procedures can and do differ. Here are a few general guidelines for pressure canning, along with details for canning common low-acid vegetables. Remember, nearly all vegetables require pressure canning to ensure food safety.

PROCESS OVERVIEW

1. Put the rack in the bottom of the canner and fill the canner with the required amount of hot water. You will not be covering the jars with water, like you did with water-bath canning. You'll probably have only about 2 or 3 inches of water in the pot, depending on the size of your canner.

2. Follow your recipe; fill and seal the jars.

3. Using a jar lifter, put the jars on the rack in the canner as you fill each one—don't wait to put them in the canner after they are all filled, as they will cool more quickly on the counter than in the canner.

4. Put the cover securely on the canner, locking as necessary, but do not put the weight on the open vent or close the petcock. Turn the temperature on high, and heat until steam flows through the vent or petcock for ten minutes to exhaust all air from inside the canner.

5. Following the manufacturer's instructions, close the petcock or put the weight on the vent. For weighted gauges, use the weight that corresponds to the pressure called for in your recipe.

6. Keep the temperature on medium-high to high as the pressure within builds. On dial-gauge canners, lower the burner temperature slightly when the pressure reaches 8 pounds per square inch (psi). This will help you regulate the pressure more easily. For dial-gauge canners, you have reached the desired pressure when the dial shows that pressure (simple enough). For weighted-gauge canners, you have reached the desired pressure when the weight sitting on the vent jiggles and hisses vigorously.

7. Once you have reached the desired pressure, begin timing. Reduce/adjust the burner temperature to maintain that pressure. For dial gauges, keep the needle at the desired pressure. For weighted gauges, follow the manufacturer's instructions, which generally tell you that the weight should jiggle or rock two to three times per minute.

8. If the pressure becomes too high, turn down the heat, but do not open the vent. If the pressure falls below the recommended amount, the food might be underprocessed. Increase the burner temperature to increase the pressure to the required amount, then begin timing again.

9. When jars have been processed for the recommended time, turn off the heat and allow the canner to cool naturally and thus depressurize. Don't try to speed up the process by running cold water over the canner. You'll know that the pressure is reduced because either the dial gauge will read zero, or, in the case of a weighted gauge, there won't be a tell-tale "hiss" when you gently move or tap the gauge. (Note: don't do this with your bare hands!) Once the pressure in the canner has been reduced to zero, carefully remove the gauge or open the petcock. Beware of escaping steam—it can give you a serious burn. Wait five minutes.

10. Carefully unlock and remove the lid from the canner base, opening the lid away from you to avoid the steam. Sometimes canners with rubber gaskets can form a suction, making them difficult to open. I've had this happen when I've let the canner cool for too long. Heating the canner slightly usually solves this problem.

11. After removing the lid, let the canner cool for ten minutes before removing the jars.

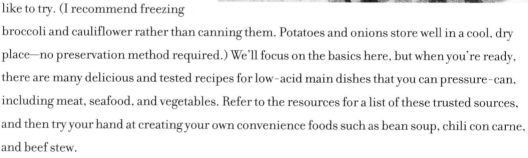

ABOUT THE RECIPES

The recipes that follow provide the details for canning many of your favorite vegetables and a few other low-acid foods that you might like to try. (I recommend freezing broccoli and cauliflower rather than canning them. Potatoes and onions store well in a cool, dry place—no preservation method required.) We'll focus on the basics here, but when you're ready, there are many delicious and tested recipes for low-acid main dishes that you can pressure-can, including meat, seafood, and vegetables. Refer to the resources for a list of these trusted sources, and then try your hand at creating your own convenience foods such as bean soup, chili con carne, and beef stew.

The processing times given apply to locations between sea level and 1,000 feet. If you live at an altitude higher than that, adjust the processing time according to "Altitude Adjustment" in the appendix. For those vegetables that you wish to blanch and remove the skins, such as tomatoes, see "All About Blanching" in the appendix. I'm providing basic recipes that have been tested and approved by the USDA, showing times for both pints and quarts, as well as pressures for both dial-gauge and weighted-gauge canners. To avoid spoilage and possible food poisoning, you must follow the recipes and instructions exactly.

Pressure Canning Recipes

For all recipes, after filling the jars to the required headspace, remove any bubbles; wipe the rims clean; adjust the lids; and process the finished jars for the stated amount of time, adjusting for altitude if necessary. Where salt is indicated, use canning salt.

Asparagus

Yield: Flexible

Ingredients:

❖ Asparagus, 3½ pounds per quart

❖ Boiling water

❖ 1 teaspoon salt per quart or ½ teaspoon salt per pint (optional)

1. Use tender spears, trimmed to remove tough ends and scales. Cut them to the desired length, then wash and drain them.

2. **To raw-pack:** Fill jars with spears, packing tightly without crushing. Add salt if desired, then add boiling water, leaving 1-inch headspace. **To hot-pack:** Cover asparagus with boiling water in a saucepan and boil for 3 minutes. Pack hot asparagus into hot jars, leaving a 1-inch headspace. Add salt if desired. Ladle boiling liquid over spears, leaving the same 1-inch headspace.

3. Process the finished jars: 30 minutes for pints and 40 minutes for quarts at 11 psi for dial-gauge canners and 10 psi for weighted-gauge canners.

Beans—Lima or Butter

Yield: Flexible

Ingredients:

❖ Beans, 4 pounds per quart

❖ Boiling water

❖ 1 teaspoon salt per quart or ½ teaspoon salt per pint (optional)

1. Select plump pods with green seeds. Wash, drain, and shell them, and then wash and drain them again.

2. **To raw-pack:** Pack the beans loosely into hot jars, leaving 1-inch headspace for pints and 1½ inches for quarts. Do not pack or shake down. Add salt if desired, then add boiling water, leaving the same headspace. **To hot-pack:** Blanch the beans in boiling water for 3 minutes (see "All About Blanching" in the appendix); then drain them and reserve the

liquid. Pack the hot beans into hot jars, leaving a 1-inch headspace. Add salt if desired. Ladle the reserved liquid, still boiling, over the beans, leaving the same 1-inch headspace.

3. Process the finished jars: 40 minutes for pints and 50 minutes for quarts at 11 psi for dial-gauge canners and 10 psi for weight-gauge canners.

Beans— Green, Wax, Snap, Hull, Purple, and Italian

Yield: Flexible

Ingredients:

* Beans, 2 pounds per quart
* Boiling water
* 1 teaspoon salt per quart or ½ teaspoon salt per pint (optional)

1. Use filled, tender, crisp pods. Wash and drain them, remove the strings, snip their ends, and leave them whole or cut/break into 2-inch pieces.

2. **To raw-pack:** Pack the beans tightly into hot jars, leaving a 1-inch headspace. Add salt if desired; then add boiling water, leaving the same 1-inch headspace. **To hot-pack:** Blanch the beans in boiling water for 5 minutes, then drain them and reserve the liquid. Pack the beans loosely into hot jars, leaving a 1-inch headspace. Add salt if desired. Ladle the reserved liquid, still boiling, over the beans, leaving the same 1-inch headspace.

3. Process the finished jars: 20 minutes for pints and 25 minutes for quarts at 11 psi for dial-gauge canners and 10 psi for weighted-gauge canners.

Beets—Whole, Cubed, or Sliced

Yield: Flexible

Ingredients:

* Beets, 3 pounds per quart
* Boiling water
* 1 teaspoon salt per quart or ½ teaspoon salt per pint (optional)

1. Use beets 1 to 2 inches in diameter. Wash and drain them; leave 2 inches of stem and tap root. Place the beets in a saucepan, cover them with water, and boil them until the skins slip off, about 15 to 20 minutes.

2. Cool the beets enough to remove their skins; then trim off the tap root and stem. Leave small beets whole. Cut medium and large beets into $\frac{1}{2}$-inch cubes or slices.

3. Pack the beets into hot jars, leaving a 1-inch headspace.

4. Add salt if desired; then add boiling water, leaving the same 1-inch headspace.

5. Process the finished jars: 30 minutes for pints and 35 minutes for quarts at 11 psi for dial-gauge canners and 10 psi for weighted-gauge canners.

Carrots—Sliced or Diced

Yield: Flexible

Ingredients:

❖ Carrots, $2\frac{1}{2}$ pounds per quart

❖ Boiling water

❖ 1 teaspoon salt per quart or $\frac{1}{2}$ teaspoon salt per pint (optional)

1. Select small carrots, 1 to $1\frac{1}{4}$ inches in diameter. Wash and peel them, wash them again, and then drain and slice or dice them.

2. **To raw-pack:** Pack the carrots tightly into hot jars, leaving a 1-inch headspace. Add salt if desired. Cover the carrots with boiling water, leaving the same 1-inch headspace.

   To hot-pack: Put the carrots in a large saucepan, cover them with boiling water, bring to a boil, and then simmer for 5 minutes. Pack the hot carrots into hot jars, leaving a 1-inch headspace. Add salt if desired. Cover the carrots with the hot cooking liquid or fresh boiling water, leaving the same 1-inch headspace.

3. Process the finished jars: 25 minutes for pints and 30 minutes for quarts at 11 psi for dial-gauge canners and 10 psi for weighted-gauge canners.

Corn—Cream Style

Yield: Flexible

Ingredients:

❖ Corn, 2½ pounds per pint. (Do not pack in quarts; the density of creamed corn makes it difficult for heat to penetrate quart-size jars.)

❖ Boiling water

❖ ½ teaspoon salt per pint (optional)

1. Select tender, freshly picked corn with slightly immature kernels. Husk the cobs and remove any silk.

2. Blanch the corn for 4 minutes in boiling water, and then cool it. Cut the kernels off the cobs, leaving the small kernels at the tips. For creamier corn, cut at the center of the kernels and scrape the cob to remove pulp and milk.

3. Measure the corn (kernels, pulp, and milk). Add 1 cup of boiling water to every 1¼ cups of corn. Heat the mixture to boiling and cook for 3 minutes. Add salt if desired.

4. Ladle the hot corn and liquid into pint jars (no quarts), leaving a 1-inch headspace.

5. Process the finished jars: 85 minutes for pints at 11 psi for dial-gauge canners and 10 psi for weighted-gauge canners.

Corn—Whole Kernel

Yield: Flexible

Ingredients:

❖ Corn, 4½ pounds per quart

❖ Boiling water

❖ 1 teaspoon salt per quart or ½ teaspoon salt per pint (optional)

1. Select tender, freshly-picked corn with slightly immature kernels. Husk the cobs, and remove any silk.

2. Blanch the corn for 3 minutes in boiling water, and then cool it. Cut the kernels off the cobs, leaving the small kernels at tips; do not scrape the cobs.

3. **To raw-pack:** Fill jars with the raw kernels, leaving a 1-inch headspace. Do not press the corn down. Add the boiling water, leaving the same 1-inch headspace. **To hot-pack:** Measure the corn. Put it in a saucepan and add 1 cup of hot water for every 4 cups of corn. Heat the mixture to boiling, and then let it simmer for 5 minutes. Add salt if desired.

Fill jars with the corn and cooking liquid, leaving a 1-inch headspace.

4. Process the finished jars: 55 minutes for pints and 85 minutes for quarts at 11 psi for dial-gauge canners and 10 psi for weighted-gauge canners.

Mixed Vegetables

Yield: 6 quarts

Ingredients:

❖ 6 cups each of sliced carrots, whole kernel corn, shelled lima beans, and crushed tomatoes

❖ Water

❖ 1 teaspoon salt per quart or ½ teaspoon salt per pint (optional)

1. Wash and prepare the vegetables following instructions for each in previous recipes.

2. Combine all vegetables in a large saucepan and add enough water to cover. Add salt if desired.

3. Bring the mixture to a boil and cook for 5 minutes. Fill hot jars with the hot vegetables and liquid, leaving a 1-inch headspace.

4. Process the finished jars: 75 minutes for pints and 90 minutes for quarts at 11 psi for dial-gauge canners and 10 psi for weighted-gauge canners.

Peas—Green or English Only

Sugar-snap and edible-pod peas are best preserved by freezing (see chapter 3).

Yield: Flexible

Ingredients:

❖ Peas, 4½ pounds per quart

❖ Boiling water

❖ 1 teaspoon salt per quart or ½ teaspoon salt per pint (optional)

1. Select pods with young, tender peas—before they have become starchy. Wash and shell the peas, then wash them again.

2. Add salt to the jars, if desired.

3. **To raw-pack:** Fill jars with the raw peas, leaving a 1-inch headspace; do not press the peas down. Cover them with boiling water to the same 1-inch headspace. **To hot-pack:** Add raw peas to a large saucepan and cover them with boiling water. Bring the mixture to a boil and cook for 2 minutes. Fill jars loosely with hot peas and cooking liquid, leaving a 1-inch headspace.

4. Process the finished jars: 40 minutes for both pints and quarts at 11 psi for dial-gauge canners and 10 psi for weighted-gauge canners.

TIP FOR PEELING WINTER
SQUASH AND PUMPKINS

Because of their tough skin, winter squash and pumpkins can be challenging to peel. After washing, microwave them on high (about 90 seconds for an average 2-pound squash) to slightly soften the skin.

Pumpkin and Winter Squash— Cubed Only

Warning: Older recipes call for canning pureed winter squash and pumpkin. This is not safe. If you want to preserve these vegetables pureed, freezing is the best method (see chapter 3).

Yield: Flexible

Ingredients:

- Pumpkin or winter squash, 2¼ pounds per quart
- Boiling water

1. Select fully ripe pumpkins and squash with hard rinds and stringless, mature meat. Wash thoroughly, cut them in half, and remove the seeds. Then peel and cut them into 1-inch cubes.

2. Place the cubes in a large saucepan, cover them with hot water, bring to a boil, and cook for 2 minutes.

3. Pack the cubes and cooking liquid into jars, leaving a 1-inch headspace.

4. Process the finished jars: 55 minutes for pints and 90 minutes for quarts at 11 psi for dial-gauge canners and 10 psi for weighted-gauge canners.

Tomatoes—Stewed

Yield: 7 pints or 3 quarts

Ingredients:

- 4 quarts tomatoes, peeled and chopped
- 1 cup celery, chopped
- 2 tablespoons sugar
- 2 teaspoons salt
- ½ cup onion, chopped coarsely
- ¼ cup green pepper, chopped coarsely

1. Wash the tomatoes, then blanch them in boiling water for 30 to 60 seconds until their skins split. Cool them, slip off the skins, and then core and chop the tomatoes.

2. Combine the tomatoes and the rest of the ingredients in a large saucepan. Bring the mixture to a boil, cover, and cook for 10 minutes, stirring to prevent sticking.

3. Ladle the hot vegetables into hot jars, leaving a 1-inch headspace.

4. Process the finished jars: 15 minutes for pints and 20 minutes for quarts at 11 psi for dial-gauge canners and 10 psi for weighted-gauge canners.

Tomato Pasta Sauce—without Meat

Note: Do not increase the proportion of onions and peppers in this recipe; this can change the acidity level.

Yield: 9 pints or 4 quarts

Ingredients:

- 30 pounds tomatoes
- 1 cup onions, finely chopped
- 6 cloves garlic, finely chopped
- 1 cup green pepper, chopped
- ¼ cup olive oil
- 4 tablespoons fresh parsley, minced
- 2 tablespoons oregano
- 4 teaspoons salt
- 2 teaspoons black pepper, freshly ground
- ¼ cup light brown sugar

1. Wash the tomatoes, then blanch them in boiling water for 30 to 60 seconds until their skins split (see "All About Blanching" in the appendix). Cool them, slip off the skins, and then core and quarter the tomatoes.

2. Place the tomatoes in a large saucepot, mash them partially to draw out some liquid, bring them to a boil, and cook uncovered for 20 minutes.

3. Press the cooked tomatoes through a sieve or food mill.

4. Sauté the onions, garlic, and peppers in olive oil until tender. Add the sautéed vegetables to the tomatoes; then add the remaining ingredients.

5. Bring the mixture to a boil, and then simmer uncovered, stirring frequently to prevent scorching, until you reach the desired consistency—the volume should be reduced by about half.

6. Ladle the sauce into hot jars, leaving a 1-inch headspace.

7. Process the finished jars: 20 minutes for pints and 25 minutes for quarts at 11 psi for dial-gauge canners and 10 psi for weighted-gauge canners.

STORE AND ENJOY

Now that the jars are canned, cooled, and snugly sealed, it's time to squirrel them away in your winter larder! Because the canning process forms an air-tight seal, there's no need to keep the bands on the jars. Remove the bands (optional), and wipe the lids and jars to remove any food particles that might remain. Dry the jars thoroughly, and then label and date each one. Some sources suggest that you mark each batch separately. For example, if you process three canner loads of applesauce (7 quarts each) on October 15, 2012, you would label the first seven quarts, "Applesauce, Batch 1, October 15, 2012." Then, if there's a problem with a jar of applesauce later in the year, you'll know to check the other six jars from Batch 1. (The truth is, in all my years of canning, I've never done this, but it's not a bad idea.) We'll talk about possible problems in "If Something Does Go Awry" on page 112.

Like soldiers standing at attention, waiting to be called into service, these canned fruits and vegetables are ready to be enjoyed.

Update your canning inventory list with the new items. While an inventory for canned products is not quite as important as it is for items that you are storing in your freezer (you have to open your freezer and let out all of the cold air to figure out what you have), it's a very simple convenience.

WHERE TO STORE

Store the jars in a dry, dark, cool (between 50 and 70 degrees Fahrenheit) place. Basements are ideal, but not everyone has a basement. Heat and sunlight will compromise the quality of your canned goods and may even cause them to spoil, so don't put them where they could reach 95 degrees Fahrenheit or in direct sunlight. Avoid attics without insulation, shelves that are close to hot pipes or furnaces, or similarly warm places. The potential for freezing is equally problematic, as the jars may crack or the lids might pop.

HOW LONG TO STORE

The USDA recommends that you use canned foods within a year. As tempting as it is to can a several-year supply—especially when you have a bumper crop—it's not recommended because after a year, the food might undergo chemical changes that could compromise its quality. You will find canning books and sites that mention storage times longer than one year; you will also talk to folks who will tell you that they've kept canned food for years. I tend to follow the USDA recommendations, but I probably wouldn't throw out my applesauce when it turned thirteen-months old.

WHEN IT'S TIME TO OPEN

When it's time to open your jar, unscrew the band (if you haven't already removed it) and pry off the lid using a can opener, being careful not to chip the lip of the jar. Recycle the lid, but do not try to reuse it. The jar, however, can be reused indefinitely, as long as it's not chipped or cracked.

If you're opening a canned vegetable, meat, or other low-acid food, the USDA recommends that you boil the food for ten minutes (for altitudes up to 1,000 feet, add 1 minute for every 1,000 feet increase in elevation) before serving it, as an extra precaution against botulism poisoning. The USDA is very cautious about home-canned food because not everyone is as careful in their processing as you and I are. If you follow the tested recipes and adhere strictly to the processing times and ingredients, you won't have any problems—but you should still follow the USDA's recommendations. This is not necessary for fruits and high-acid foods; they are perfectly safe to eat without first cooking them.

While these canned tomatoes might look great sitting in the sun, they won't fare well if kept there. They should be relocated to a cool, dark area for storage.

If your canned food doesn't come out of the jar looking as perfect and delicious as this homemade applesauce, a number of culprits could be responsible.

IF SOMETHING DOES GO AWRY

As with any new skill or craft, you're bound to have some concerns or questions about your home-canned foods. Sometimes the canned product doesn't turn out as well as we would like, but it is still perfectly safe to eat. Check out the next section, "What Can the Matter Be?" for some suggestions for next time.

While it is highly unlikely that your canned food will spoil, you need to know what to look for and how to handle it. I apologize if some of this section sounds like a page from a nuclear warfare manual, but this falls into the "better safe than sorry" category.

WHAT CAN THE MATTER BE?

Sometimes, despite our best efforts and excellent recipes, our canning outcome is less than perfect. Below are some of the common complaints/concerns of novice canners. If you are in doubt, don't hesitate to call your local Agricultural Extension Service for guidance. They are wonderful, friendly folks who are there to help you.

❖ **Jars don't seal.** A number of things can cause this, including a chip in the jar rim, a fleck of food on the rim, and not preparing and/or processing the food long enough. If this happens, you can reprocess the food within twenty-four hours, or just refrigerate it and use it within the next day or so.

❧ **Liquid has "escaped" from the jar, leaving too much headspace and food uncovered.** First, don't open the jar to replace the liquid. The food inside is fine, though it may turn a bit brown on top. The cause is most likely not that the liquid escaped, but that there wasn't enough liquid to begin with. This happens more frequently with raw packing than with hot packing. This could also be caused by hidden air bubbles that escaped during processing, causing the liquid level to drop. Raw food will shrink more than hot or cooked food, so that will lower the liquid level. Operator failure is also a possibility. If you don't maintain consistent pressure in a pressure canner, if you don't keep your jars covered with 1 to 2 inches of water in a water-bath canner, or if you try to force-cool your pressure canner, you can lose liquid from inside the jars. Lastly, starchy foods, by their nature, just absorb liquids more than other types. There's nothing you can do to prevent liquid loss for them.

❧ **Brown discoloration on the food at the top of the jar.** This is not necessarily a sign of spoilage but rather of oxidation or enzyme action—especially common in foods that are susceptible to oxidation, such as apples. Pretreat as recommended with ascorbic acid. Make sure that you got all of the air bubbles out, that you've filled the jar with the right amount of water, and that you processed it long enough to stop the enzyme action.

❧ **Fruit darkens after removing it from the jar.** Enzymes are probably the culprit here. This doesn't affect food safety; it just means that you didn't process the food quite long enough. Remember: don't start counting your processing time until the water in your water-bath canner reaches a full, rolling boil.

❧ **Fruit changes color in the jar.** Some canned fruits (for example, apples, pears, and peaches) undergo a natural chemical transformation when cooked, and they can change to pink, red, blue, or purple. This is normal.

❧ **Crystals appear in grapes and grape products.** In both cases, this is natural and harmless. In grapes, tartaric acid causes the crystals. You can help by letting the juice stand overnight so that the sediment drops to the bottom. Avoid that sediment when you are ladling the juice into jars.

❧ **Black spots appear on the inside of the metal lid.** As bothersome as this might look, it's not a problem. There are naturally occurring substances in some foods that simply deposit themselves on the underside of the lid. No worries.

❧ **Jars initially seal and then unseal; jars seep; lids bulge; or food bubbles and smells foul, is moldy, or has an unnatural color.** This tells you that there's a food safety problem. Do not touch or eat the food!

HOW WILL I KNOW IF MY FOOD HAS SPOILED?

Before you open a jar of canned food, look at it carefully for signs that something's amiss. Most of the time, there will be a visible hint that have a problem. Some of the more common ones are:

❖ Bulging lids or food seeping from the lid

❖ Food or liquid spurts out when the jar is opened

❖ Mold—anywhere, in any amount, and in any form

❖ Fermentation

❖ Cloudy liquid or shriveled food. (Sometimes cloudiness indicates spoilage, but it can also be due to minerals in your water or fillers in your salt. Use soft water and canning or pickling salt.)

❖ Significant and unnatural changes in the color and texture of the food—for example, a very dark color, a slimy feel, or an unpleasant smell. Remember, however, that after canning, all foods will be softer and probably won't have the intense color of its fresh counterpart.

Notice that I said "most of the time." The exception is botulism. At the risk of scaring and scarring you completely, most times, foods that have spoiled because of botulism will have nice, tight seals (remember, botulism is anaerobic and doesn't like oxygen). Such foods may show no signs of spoilage. All the more reason to follow pressure-canning instructions religiously.

WHAT DO I DO WITH MY SPOILED FOOD?

While this doesn't happen very often (honestly, *never* for me in thirty-some years of canning, just to give you a probability) **if you suspect that the food has spoiled, or you question whether a low-acid food was properly processed, don't think twice—don't eat or taste it! Just get rid of it!**

If it's a low-acid food or tomato product, one that could possibly have botulism, you'll need to do this carefully so that no person or creature could be exposed to it. You cannot simply put it down the garbage disposal, or in the compost pile, trash, or even toilet. You will need to detoxify it to render any potential botulism spores harmless. Do not open or empty the jar. Put the entire jar with the lid in a large saucepan, add water to cover the jar with 1 to 2 inches of water, cover the saucepan with a lid, and boil the jar for thirty minutes. Don't allow any liquid or spoiled food to splash outside the saucepan. After thirty minutes, let the whole thing cool, and dispose of everything but the saucepan: that means the water, jar, lid, and food. Pour the boiled water down the drain, put the closed jar in a plastic trash bag, and place it in the garbage. Then, clean everything that touched the food using a disinfectant solution made up of 1 part chlorine bleach and 5 parts water (use a disposable wash cloth or sponge).

If you have concerns or questions, don't hesitate to call your local Cooperative Extension Service for guidance.

The University of Nebraska at Lincoln maintains a website with information and links to Cooperative Extension Service locations across the country. This is a very helpful page to bookmark in your online browser: http://lancaster.unl.edu/office/locate.shtml.

WHAT'S NEXT?

I can't end this chapter talking about botulism and detoxifying! Now that you've learned how to can fruits and vegetables, don't stop here. Water-bath canning is the perfect way to preserve your favorite jams, jellies, conserves, marmalades, and other soft spreads. Or try your hand at pickles, relish, or sauerkraut. Just turn the page!

CHAPTER 5

Jams, Jellies, and More

Now for the fun stuff—not that we haven't been having fun with freezing and canning, but we're now crossing the line from utility to artistry, from the necessities to the niceties. Yes, it's very gratifying and convenient to have your larder filled with summer's bountiful overstock of beans, tomatoes, corn, applesauce, and peaches, but it's a decadent joy in January to savor whole-wheat toast with butter and homemade red-raspberry jam. And what's more fun than to present your friends and family with handcrafted jams, jellies, or fruit butters as holiday gifts?

In earlier chapters, I made ardent arguments about the nutrition and value of your home-preserved foods. We can now back down some on the nutritional aspect and emphasize the value. The gift of homemade jam—the fresh taste, vibrant hue, and sweetness of summer crafted with love and caring—is priceless. There *is* artistry in the making of sweet and savory spreads. They sparkle with color in their pretty little glass jars. Dress them up with holiday ribbons and labels, and it becomes hard to give them away and even harder to think of opening them. But when you do, and your recipient takes that first bite, she will never go back to store-bought again. Best of all, this beauty and flavor is well within your reach, even if you've never canned before.

SO MANY CHOICES!

There are many choices when it comes to fruit spreads. In this chapter, we'll keep our attention on fruit-based soft spreads—those that rely on fruit, acid, pectin, and sugar for their texture and, to some extent, for their preservation. There are many tasty recipes out there for jams, jellies, and other soft spreads that use vegetables as well as fruits. There are also savory vegetable-based spreads such as ketchup and salsas, which we'll discuss in chapter 6 along with pickled foods.

We're all familiar with jams and jellies, but let's look at all of our choices. It's funny how people can be very polarized about their preferences. It's almost like politics—you don't serve jelly to a "jam person." The differences revolve mostly around consistency rather than ingredients. We don't list it, but you can assume that sugar is added to most of these.

❖ **Fruit butter.** Fruit butter, such as apple butter, is made from fruit pulp and sometimes spices that are cooked slowly to a thick, smooth consistency similar to ketchup.

❖ **Conserve.** Think jam, only chunkier and with a variety of ingredients. A conserve is made using a combination of fruits, nuts, raisins, and sometimes spices that are cooked until the conserve is thick enough to mound up.

Jellies, jams, conserves, and more! There are so many ways to enjoy summer fruits (and vegetables) year-round.

❖ **Jam.** Jam is made from whole fruit (except large seeds or pits) that has been mashed or chopped finely. The product is a thick spread that is not clear and will not hold its shape.

❖ **Jelly.** Jelly is the opposite of jam in that it is made from only the strained fruit juice, ideally with no hint of pulp, so that it's crystal clear. Also unlike jam, jelly has a slightly gelled consistency so that it will hold its shape yet spread easily on bread.

❖ **Marmalade**. If jelly is the opposite of jam, marmalade might be the compromise. A marmalade contains small pieces or bits of fruit (most often citrus and citrus rind) suspended in a transparent jelly. The consistency is closer to that of a jam.

❖ **Preserve**. This appropriately named spread is made from large chunks of fruit or whole fruit (rather than the mashed or finely chopped fruit found in jam) that is "preserved" in a medium to thick sugar syrup. The fruit pieces keep their shape and become transparent, shiny, and tender. More so than some other spreads, preserves do not hold their shape on a spoon.

USING FROZEN FRUIT FOR JAM

For other types of home food preservation, freshness is very important. This is also true for soft spreads, but in this case "fresh" can mean either freshly picked *or* frozen when freshly picked. Frozen fruits and fruit juices work just fine as long as the fruit was high quality when you froze it. Using frozen fruit is especially helpful if you can't get a full recipe's worth of fruit in one picking. For example, I grow red raspberries in my garden. When the season starts, I might only get a half-pint or a pint a day—not nearly enough for a recipe of my favorite raspberry jam. I just pick what I can each day and *immediately* rinse them, carefully dry them, and then stick them in the freezer. When I get enough in the freezer, I take them out and make my jam.

Freezing soft berries, such as raspberries or strawberries, will weaken their cell structure and help release the juice. In fact, freezing may be sufficient to extract the juice—no cooking required.

THE ESSENTIALS

All of the soft spreads we will discuss in this chapter share four essential components: fruit, pectin, acid, and some type of sweetener. The combination of these four main ingredients enables the soft spread to achieve the desired consistency—to use the jelly-maker's lingo, they "gel" or "set." What form these components take, where they come from, and how you mix them together determines both the complexity of the process and the end product.

The white haze that you see on the skins of some fruits is natural pectin. As the fruit ripens, the pectin diminishes.

FRUIT

The variety of fruits that are suitable for making soft spreads is nearly infinite. In this book, we'll focus on some of the easier ones to use, and certainly on those that are likely to be local, but if you're adventuresome, you can find recipes for more exotic ingredients such as kiwi, pomegranate, and figs, not to mention interesting combinations such as cinnamon with grapes or basil with bananas.

When selecting your fruit, you'll want it, as always, to be fresh and flavorful. An important factor is ripeness. You definitely do not want fruit that is past its peak, but in some cases, you may want fruit that is a tad on the green side or, more likely, fully ripe fruit with a small amount of underripe fruit. The reason here is the amount of natural pectin (a substance that helps with the gelling process) in the fruit. Different fruits contain different amounts of pectin, some parts of fruit contain more pectin than others, and underripe fruit has more pectin than fully ripe fruit. During a time when folks needed to rely solely on the amount of natural pectin in a fruit, this was a bigger factor than it is for us today. Now, you mostly choose your fruit based on your taste preferences, the availability of fruit, or the type of spread that you'd like to make. The pectin issue, as we'll soon see, can be easily solved.

GREAT "GREEN" SPREADS

Think local, think natural, and think inexpensive. If we're looking at carbon footprints and sustainable food sources, just look around for great jam and jelly sources right in your own backyard. The following are some good options:

❖ **Mulberry jam or jelly.** In some parts of the country, mulberry bushes grow into trees that bear large, sweet, juicy berries. Some folks think of them as a nuisance, but they're delicious and often a free source for your "jam sessions."

❖ **Crab apple jelly.** Crab apples are in almost the same situation as the mulberry—although they aren't very good for eating, they make a lovely jelly.

❖ **Beach rose or rose hip jelly or jam.** The beach rose (*Rosa rugosa*) is a variety of rose that produces various colored flowers with a hip (seed pod) that is large and turns bright red in the fall. The hip is about the size of a cherry tomato and can be used in both jelly and jam. Go to any beach-resort gift shop and you'll pay dearly for beach rose jam. But where they grow wild, beach rose hips are yours for the picking.

❖ **Wild blueberry or wild grape jam or jelly.** Go foraging! It's fun and great exercise. When you gather wild fruit, you'll have to deal with smaller fruit, but you'll be rewarded with a flavor that's distinct from jam made using their cultivated and coddled city cousins. If you're not familiar with wild fruit, there are books and online resources that can help you safely identify them. Make sure, however, not to venture onto private property—no matter how perfect those berries look.

PECTIN

Pectin is a naturally occurring substance (a complex set of polysaccharides, if you care) found in the nonwoody portions of many plants, especially fruits. Without getting into a chemistry lesson, suffice it to say that pectin combines with the water, sugar, and acid in the fruit spread (either added or naturally occurring) and causes it to thicken, or gel. Because the water is chemically bound by the sugar, acid, and pectin, it's not very available to support microorganisms that cause spoilage, thus helping to preserve the soft spread. (Despite what your grandmother may have done, all jams, jellies, and soft

Pears have negligable amounts of pectin, so recipes that use them will also require a commercial pectin product.

spreads must be preserved by water-bath canning to ensure safe preservation.)

Some fruits, such as sour apples, sour blackberries, citrus skins, currants, quinces, and cranberries, are high in pectin. Some others, such as ripe apples, cherries, ripe blackberries, and grapefruit, are low in pectin. Still others, such as apricots, blueberries, peaches, and pears, have negligible amounts of pectin. Generally, the peel and the core of fruit contain the most pectin, which is why some recipes call for adding these parts.

The good news here is that you can add pectin when making your spread to supplement the fruit's natural supply. For some fruits, this may be the only way to get the soft spread to gel. There are several options for adding pectin in both dry and liquid form, as we'll discuss in a moment. Follow your recipe's instructions for the type and amount of pectin required. The different types are not interchangeable and are usually added to the fruit at different times.

With citrus fruit, the pectin comes from the peels (the fruit has very little), which is why many recipes require adding peel.

My first choice has always been commercially prepared pectin. While I'm very concerned about cooking naturally and without additives, I use regular commercially prepared pectin without hesitation. It's generally made from apple pectin, so it's natural and safe, plus it's easy to use, does not affect the flavor, allows you to cook your fruit for a shorter length of time (giving the spread a fresher flavor and somewhat more nutritious content), and, most importantly, takes the risk and guesswork out of jam- and jelly-making. If this is your first foray into soft spreads, using commercially prepared pectin is a practically foolproof way to produce a delicious jam.

Many folks applaud the newer low- and no-sugar, freezer-variety pectins. With these, you do have the benefit of significantly lowering the amount of sugar that you use,

Commercial pectins are often made using apple pectin, so you don't have to worry about what's going into your soft spreads.

which is a boon if you are on a sugar-restrictive diet. Despite these arguments, I still prefer regular powdered pectin, mainly because it's all-natural, it has no additives or preservatives, and I get consistently good results. There's one major exception here: low-sugar methoxyl pectin, which is also all-natural and has no preservatives. It is not as readily available as some of the familiar brands of pectin, but it is a good option if you want a low-sugar spread.

The pectin that occurs naturally in fruits can only be coached out by boiling quickly. Except for fruit butters, which don't rely on pectin for their consistency, you won't find recipes calling for slow cooking. This is an important point to remember if you choose recipes for soft spreads that don't require added pectin. The bottom line here is that you'll need pectin in some shape or form in your soft-spread recipe.

PECTIN POSSIBILITIES

When you see them listed, the forms and types of pectin products can be a bit confusing. My suggestion, if you're just starting out, is to pick a basic recipe and a basic commercially manufactured pectin and stick with them until you're ready to explore.

ACID

The acid in soft spreads is necessary for a number of reasons: it adds flavor, helps with gelling, and also helps with the preservation of the spread because it lowers the pH level. If the fruit that you are using is low in natural acid, the recipe will call for the addition of lemon juice or (rarely) vinegar. Always add the exact amounts called for to ensure a proper gel or set.

BOTTLED IS BEST

The acidity of freshly squeezed lemon juice is variable, depending on the lemon variety and harvest conditions, whereas bottled lemon juice is produced to consistent acidity standards. In recipes that specify bottled lemon juice, use only bottled juice to ensure the proper level of acidity. If the type of lemon juice is not specified, you may use either freshly squeezed or bottled.

SWEETENER

Sugar (in its various forms) is needed to help the spread gel and to help with the preservation. When the recipe calls for sugar, you can use either cane or beet sugar. Depending upon your taste or nutritional preferences, you can substitute honey or nonsugar alternatives or use a recipe that calls for no added sugar.

* **Honey.** Select only a light, mild-flavored variety of honey to avoid overpowering the natural taste of the fruit. For a recipe with no added pectin, substitute no more than half of the sugar for an equal amount of honey. If the recipe calls for added pectin, you can substitute up to 2 cups of the required sugar with the same amount of honey.

* **Nonsugar substitutes.** Use these only if you have a tested recipe that specifically calls for artificial sugar. There are several commercial pectins designed to work with artificial sweeteners.

* **No sugar.** Fruits that contain high amounts of natural sugar (fructose) and high amounts of pectin can be made into "all fruit" spreads. These can be tricky, and there are few recipes available for these.

Many folks prefer to sweeten their spreads with hony, but be choosy with the type. Strongly flavored honey can overpower the fruit flavor.

OTHER INGREDIENTS

Besides these four basic ingredients, some recipes call for spices, flavorings, nuts, dried fruits, and other interesting amendments. Follow recipes carefully, paying attention to the timing for adding these ingredients, because they can overpower the fruit's natural flavor.

EQUIPMENT

The good news about making fruit spreads is that you probably have most of the equipment that you'll need to begin. If you're planning to preserve the spreads for later use, you'll need either suitable freezer containers (see chapter 3) for freezer jam, or water-bath canning equipment and jars (see chapter 4) for canned spreads. Beyond the canning equipment, here's what you'll need:

❖ An 8- to 10-quart pot with either an enamel or stainless-steel interior; a pot with a heavy, flat bottom and tall sides will keep the syrup from boiling over (for me, an 8-quart pot is perfect)

❖ Large pans, bowls, a colander, a masher, knives, and a cutting board for washing and preparing fruit

❖ Measuring cups and a food scale (most recipes will specify pounds of fruit, then translate that into cups of prepared fruit)

❖ A long-handled, stainless-steel spoon for stirring

❖ A long-handled skimming or slotted spoon for removing foam from syrup

❖ A candy/jelly thermometer (be sure to calibrate it)

❖ A jelly bag for separating pulp and seeds from juice, which can be purchased premade or made easily from unbleached, thoroughly washed muslin; as an alternative, you can place several layers of cheesecloth in a colander (see "The Art of the Jelly Bag" in the appendix)

❖ A spice bag for adding seasoning in some recipes

❖ A timer or clock

Most kitchens already have all the equipment needed to make jellies, jams, and such.

WHERE AND HOW TO BEGIN

By now, you should have a pretty good idea of the types of soft spreads that you can make and the basic ingredients involved. In the world of making and preserving soft spreads exists a range of choices and levels of difficulty. Some of the choices revolve around the type of spread and the ingredients, while others are based on whether or not you'll use added pectin. The first step is deciding *what you want to make* (for example, strawberry freezer jam, grape jelly, orange marmalade); you'll then decide if you want to use a recipe *with or without added pectin*. If this is your first foray, I suggest starting in order of difficulty—for instance, strawberry freezer jam, then strawberry cooked jam with added pectin, then jellies with added pectin. Once you feel comfortable with these, there's no stopping you. Conserves, marmalades, and preserves are nothing to fear; they just require a few more ingredients and a little more preparation and cooking.

WHAT TO DO AND NOT TO DO

For all recipes, measure ingredients accurately and use the exact amount of fruit, sugar, pectin, and lemon juice called for. It can be tempting to reduce the amount of sugar, but the proportions are very important to get a proper set. If you want to reduce the amount of sugar or use a sugar substitute, select a variety of pectin that will allow you to do that.

When measuring the sugar, put it into a bowl or a measured, wide-mouthed pitcher so that you can add it quickly (all at once) to the other boiling ingredients.

PREPARING YOUR FRUIT: MASH AND MEASURE

With all of the kitchen gadgets available today, you might need to dig deep to pull out your old potato masher, but that's really what you want for crushing berries, such as strawberries, blueberries, and raspberries, or other soft fruit. Unless you have a very sophisticated food processor that gives you a great deal of control over the texture, keep your blender or food processor in the cabinet. These create a puree, which will be just too smooth and not very interesting for a jam. Blenders and such can break down the pectin, which we know that the jam needs for a good set.

When mashing the fruit with the potato masher, always mash just one layer at a time to achieve a consistent texture. Measure the fruit exactly. If the recipe calls for 2 pints of dry strawberries or 2 cups mashed, you must have 2 cups. Most recipes say to add a bit of water or juice if you come up short on the fruit measurement.

Is It Jam Yet?

One concern with making soft spreads is whether you have cooked the mixture enough so that it will gel or set. However, this is only a concern if you're making a soft spread without added commercial pectin. Recipes that include commercially prepared pectin give specific cooking times; if you follow the recipe, you are pretty much guaranteed success. If you're making your soft spread without added pectin, there are three accepted methods:

* **Spoon or sheeting test (use only for jelly).** Using a cool metal spoon, dip out a little of the boiling syrup, moving the spoon away from the steam so that it can cool. Slowly turn the spoon so that the syrup runs off the side. If the syrup is very thin and runs easily, it's not done. As it begins to form drops that stick together, it's getting closer. It should be done when the drops form a sheet that slips off the spoon. I find this test pretty subjective and think that the next two are more reliable and measurable.

* **Candy thermometer.** Using a candy thermometer, determine the boiling point for water (at sea level with an accurate thermometer, it will be 212 degrees Fahrenheit). The gelling point will be 8 degrees higher (220 degrees Fahrenheit, in this case). When the syrup reaches that temperature, remove it from heat. If you are compulsive like me, you'll also perform the next test.

* **Cold plate.** Put a few drops of the syrup on a very cold plate and stick it in the freezer until it's cool. If it's nicely gelled (it will separate when you run your finger through it), then remove the syrup from the heat.

Be precise and patient when timing, following instructions exactly. Wait the stated times for soft spreads to cool before storing the jars. Most soft spreads don't reach their desired consistency for twenty-four hours after processing, some longer.

Be flexible and patient, especially if you're making jams without added pectin. Many factors, such as the size of the pot, humidity, and the amount of moisture in the fruit, can affect how long your syrup needs to cook. Don't panic if it takes longer to reach a gel state than the recipe suggested. Follow and trust the gel tests and candy thermometer (see the "Is It Jam Yet?" sidebar).

Make just one batch (one recipe's worth) of jam at a time. This ties in with the "be patient" part, which I acknowledge is difficult. As tempting as it is to try to expedite the process, most recipes—particularly those that use commercially prepared pectin—will caution you to make just one batch at a time.

LET'S MAKE JAM!

This section includes all of the details that you'll need to make what will soon become your favorite soft spread. I've divided the soft spreads by type, generally from the easiest to the most complex: freezer jams and jellies, soft spreads made with added pectin, soft spreads made without added pectin, and fruit butters. Because most marmalades, conserves, and preserves are made without added pectin, instructions and recipes for them are covered in that category.

Stainless steel or enamel-coated pots are best for making soft spreads because they don't react to the acid in fruit.

Water-bath canning is the only safe method of long-term preservation for soft spreads (not including freezer-type spreads). The canning process is the same as we covered in chapter 4, but for convenience, I'll provide you with a recap of the basics under "Canning Soft Spreads" following the recipes.

MAKING FREEZER JAMS AND JELLIES WITH ADDED PECTIN

Freezer jams are wonderfully delicious and simple to make. Because there's very little cooking involved, it's almost like eating the fresh fruit. The downside is that, obviously, you will need to keep the jam in the freezer. This makes them a bit more expensive to store (electricity-wise) and more difficult to give as gifts. In addition, freezer jams tend to be heavy on sugar. You will always need added pectin to make freezer jam. Freezer jam-style pectin is now available, but you can also use regular pectin (though it will require more sugar).

Like carpenters say: "measure twice, cut once." It's very important that you measure your ingredients accurately.

PROCESS OVERVIEW

You should follow the instructions that come with the pectin that you purchase or use a recipe that's specifically intended for freezer jam, but here's the basic process:

1. Thoroughly wash and rinse your freezer containers. Straight-sided plastic containers in 1- and 2-cup sizes are best, but you can also use glass jelly jars.
2. Measure the exact amount of sugar called for in your recipe.
3. Prepare the fruit (chop finely or crush one layer at a time) or fruit juice, and measure out the exact amount called for.
4. If using dry pectin and required by the recipe, add lemon to the fruit.
5. Add sugar to the fruit/juice and let it stand for 10 minutes.
6. Dissolve the dry pectin in water and boil for a minute, or, if using liquid pectin, mix it with lemon and water.
7. Add the pectin/water mixture to the fruit/sugar mixture and stir constantly for 3 minutes.
8. Put the jam/jelly in your freezer containers, being sure to allow a ½-inch headspace for expansion when frozen.
9. Let the mixture stand (either at room temperature or in the refrigerator—check your instructions) until set, usually 24 hours.
10. Label and date your homemade jam. Store it in the refrigerator for up to three weeks or in the freezer for up to one year.
11. When ready to use the frozen jam or jelly, thaw it in the refrigerator.

SORRY, GRANDMA

Despite what your mother, my mother, and everyone's grandmother did, the only approved method for preserving soft spreads is water-bath canning. Yes, I grew up with paraffin wax on the top of my mother's jams and have lived to write this book, but I won't use that method because of the risks of spoilage. Plus, it's not really any easier than water-bath canning. Without going into details, working with melted paraffin is pretty tricky. The other method commonly used was to forgo the water bath and simply put the boiling jam into the hot jars, put on the lids and bands, turn the jars upside down to theoretically kill all of the microorganisms that might have clung to the bottom of the lids, and then put the jars right side up and let them cool on the counter. When using this "inversion" method, if the boiling jam was hot enough, physics probably caused the lids to seal, but maybe not, and maybe the jam wasn't hot enough to kill the microorganisms, and maybe...you get the idea. There are just too many maybes here. Because of the high acid and sugar content, most soft spreads require a relatively short water-bath processing time, so why take chances?

Freezer Jam and Jelly Recipes

Blackberry, Blueberry, or Red or Black Raspberry Freezer Jam

Yield: 6 half-pints

Ingredients:

❖ 3 cups crushed berries (2¼ pounds fruit)

❖ 5¼ cups sugar

❖ 2 tablespoons lemon juice

❖ 1 box (1.75-ounce) dry pectin

❖ ¾ cup water

Follow the instructions in the process overview under "Making Freezer Jams and Jellies."

Grape Freezer Jelly

Yield: 5 half-pints

Ingredients:

❖ 2 cups grape juice (2 pounds fruit) or bottled concord grape juice—not from concentrate

❖ 4 cups sugar

❖ 1 pouch (3-ounce) liquid pectin

❖ 2 tablespoons water

Follow the instructions in the process overview under "Making Freezer Jams and Jellies."

Grape freezer jelly may take up to a week in the refrigerator to set.

Peach Freezer Jam

Yield: 5 half-pints

Ingredients:

❖ 2¼ cups finely chopped or mashed peaches (2 pounds fruit)

❖ 4½ cups sugar

❖ 1 tablespoon lemon juice

❖ 1 box (1.75-ounce) dry pectin

Follow the instructions in the process overview under "Making Freezer Jams and Jellies."

Strawberry Freezer Jam

Yield: 5 half-pints

Ingredients:

❖ 2 cups mashed strawberries
   (2 pounds fruit)

❖ 4 cups sugar

❖ 2 tablespoons lemon juice

❖ 1 box (1.75-ounce) dry pectin

Follow the instructions in the process overview under "Making Freezer Jams and Jellies."

MAKING COOKED SOFT SPREADS WITH ADDED PECTIN

Making cooked spreads using added pectin is almost as easy as making freezer jam. The results are delicious and dependable. Many good recipes are provided with packaged pectin. If you use one of these, follow the steps and ingredients exactly. The processes for making jams, jellies, and other soft spreads using added pectin are similar, except for preparing the juice for jelly (see "The Art of the Jelly Bag" in the appendix). Because the timing for adding dry pectin differs from that for liquid pectin, I've included the steps for each.

PROCESS OVERVIEW FOR RECIPES WITH DRY PECTIN

1. Prepare your containers and water-bath canner.

2. Measure the sugar and set it aside.

3. Prepare the fruit, measure the fruit exactly according to the recipe, and add lemon juice if called for. When preparing fruit for jams, crush one layer of fruit at a time. If making jelly, cook the fruit and extract the juice (see "The Art of the Jelly Bag" in the appendix).

4. Pour the fruit/juice into a saucepot and stir in the dry pectin, mixing it in thoroughly. Add about ½ teaspoon of butter or margarine to reduce foaming if desired.

5. Bring the mixture quickly to a full boil (a rolling boil that can't be stirred down). Add the sugar all at once, stirring well to dissolve it, and then return the juice to a full, rolling boil. Be careful here, as the cooked fruit and sugar is now a very hot syrup and can easily spatter.

6. Boil for 1 minute, stirring constantly. Time this precisely from when the mixture returned to a full boil.

7. Remove the pot from the heat and skim off any foam. Ladle the fruit/juice into the prepared jars, leaving the required headspace, and remove any air bubbles if necessary.

8. Now that you're ready to process the jars, see "Canning Soft Spreads" on page 149 for processing instructions.

PROCESS OVERVIEW FOR RECIPES WITH LIQUID PECTIN

1. Prepare your containers and water-bath canner.

2. Measure the sugar and set it aside. Prepare the fruit, measure it exactly according to the recipe, and add lemon juice if called for. When preparing fruit for jams, crush one layer of fruit at a time. If making jelly, cook the fruit and extract the juice (see "The Art of the Jelly Bag" in the appendix).

3. Combine your measured fruit/juice in a saucepot with the sugar. Add ½ teaspoon butter or margarine to reduce foaming if desired.

4. Bring the mixture to a full boil. Add the liquid pectin quickly.

5. Bring back to a full boil and boil hard for 1 minute. Time this precisely from when the mixture returned to a full boil.

6. Remove the pot from the heat and skim off any foam. Ladle the fruit/juice into prepared jars, leaving the required headspace, and remove any air bubbles if necessary.

7. Now that you're ready to process the jars, see "Canning Soft Spreads" on page 149 for processing instructions.

WHAT ABOUT THE FOAM?

Once you start making jam, you'll see that, depending upon the fruit you are using, foam is a force to be reckoned with. Boiling syrup makes bubbles aplenty, which will turn to sticky foam. Nearly every recipe will instruct you to skim the foam from the boiling syrup, and some will tell you to add a bit of butter or oil to prevent foam from occurring at all.

The foam is perfectly safe to eat, though it might not appear very appetizing. You do, however, want to skim off as much as you can before you ladle your hot spread into your jars. The air inside the bubbles can create extra headspace, which will prevent the jars from sealing as tightly as they would normally, so your jam might not keep as long. I simply skim off the foam, save it in the refrigerator, and use it like regular jam. From a couple of batches of jam, I'll usually have a cup or so of foam. It tastes just like the jam, only light and airy. Trust me—it won't last long!

Recipes for Soft Spreads Using Pectin

For all recipes, after filling jars to the required headspace, remove any bubbles, wipe the rims clean, adjust the lids, and process the jars for the stated time, making allowances as necessary for altitude (see "Altitude Adjustment" in the appendix).

JAMS

Apricot Jam

Yield: 8 half-pints

Ingredients:

❖ 3½ pounds apricots, chopped to yield 5 cups

❖ ¼ cup lemon juice

❖ 7 cups sugar

❖ 1 box (1.75-ounce) dry pectin

Follow the instructions in "Process Overview for Recipes with Dry Pectin." Leave a ¼-inch headspace. Process the finished jars for 10 minutes.

Blueberry Jam

Yield: 6 half-pints

Ingredients:

❖ 3 pints blueberries, crushed to yield 4 cups

❖ 2 tablespoons lemon juice

❖ 4 cups sugar

❖ 1 box (1.75-ounce) dry pectin

Follow the instructions in "Process Overview for Recipes with Dry Pectin." Leave a ¼-inch headspace. Process the finished jars for 10 minutes.

Chocolate Red-Raspberry Jam

This jam may be soft and can be used equally well as jam or a delicious sauce for sundaes.

Yield: 6 half-pints

Ingredients:

* ½ cups unsweetened cocoa powder (sifted)
* 2 quarts (approximately) red raspberries, crushed to yield 4½ cups
* 4 tablespoons lemon juice
* 6¾ cups sugar
* 1 box (1.75-ounce) dry pectin

1. Combine the cocoa and pectin in a glass bowl and set aside.

2. Sieve half of the raspberries, if desired, to remove some of the seeds (resulting measurement must still equal 4½ cups). Place the crushed raspberries and lemon juice in a large saucepan and whisk in the cocoa/pectin mixture until completely dissolved. Bring to a boil over high heat, stirring constantly.

3. Add the sugar all at once and return the mixture to a full, rolling boil, stirring constantly. Boil hard for 1 minute.

4. Remove from heat, skim off the foam, and ladle into prepared jars, leaving a ¼-inch headspace. Process the finished jars for 10 minutes.

Grape Jam

Yield: 9 half-pints

Ingredients:

* 4 pounds Concord grapes, prepared to yield 6 cups
* 7 cups sugar
* 1 box (1.75-ounce) dry pectin

1. Squeeze the grapes to remove the pulp from the skin.

2. Finely chop the skins and set them aside.

3. Add 1 cup of water to the pulp and cook it slowly for 5 minutes, covered.

4. Sieve the pulp to remove any seeds.

5. Add the chopped skins to the pulp.

6. Continue with the instructions in "Process Overview for Recipes with Dry Pectin." Leave a ¼-inch headspace. Process the finished jars for 10 minutes.

Raspberry Jam

Yield: 8 half-pints

Ingredients:

❖ 2 quarts (approximately) red or black raspberries, crushed to yield 4 cups

❖ 6½ cups sugar

❖ 1 pouch (3-ounce) liquid pectin

1. If desired, sieve half of the berries to reduce the amount of seeds (the total amount of pulp must equal 4 cups regardless).

2. Continue with the instructions in "Process Overview for Recipes with Liquid Pectin." Leave a ¼-inch headspace. Process the finished jars for 10 minutes.

Strawberry Jam

Yield: 8 half-pints

Ingredients:

❖ 2 quarts strawberries, crushed to yield 5 cups

❖ 7 cups sugar

❖ ¼ cups lemon juice

❖ 1 box (1.75-ounce) dry pectin

Follow the instructions in "Process Overview for Recipes with Dry Pectin." Leave a ¼-inch headspace. Process the finished jars for 10 minutes.

JELLIES

Blackberry Jelly

Yield: 6 half-pints

Ingredients:

❖ 3 quarts blackberries

❖ 7½ cups sugar

❖ 2 pouches (3 ounces each) liquid pectin

1. Render the 3 quarts of blackberries to achieve 4 cups of juice, following the instructions found in "The Art of the Jelly Bag" in the appendix.

2. Follow the instructions in "Process Overview for Recipes with Liquid Pectin." Leave a ¼-inch headspace. Process the finished jars for 10 minutes.

Crab Apple Jelly

Yield: 7 half-pints

Ingredients:

- 4 pounds crab apples (about 56 crab apples)
- 5 cups water
- 7 cups sugar
- 1 box (1.75-ounce) dry pectin

1. Render the 4 pounds of crab apples and 5 cups of water to achieve 5 cups of juice, following the instructions found in "The Art of the Jelly Bag" in the appendix.
2. Continue with the instructions in "Process Overview for Recipes with Dry Pectin."
3. Leave a 1/4-inch headspace. Process the finished jars for 10 minutes.

Plum Jelly

Yield: 8 half-pints

Ingredients:

- 5 pounds plums
- 1½ cups water
- 7½ cups sugar
- 1 box (1.75-ounce) dry pectin

1. Render the 5 pounds of plums and 1½ cups of water to achieve 5½ cups of juice, following the instructions found in "The Art of the Jelly Bag" in the appendix.
2. Follow the instructions in "Process Overview for Recipes with Dry Pectin." Leave a 1/4-inch headspace. Process the finished jars for 10 minutes.

Rhubarb Conserve

Yield: 7 half-pints

Ingredients:

* 2 pounds rhubarb (4 cups chopped)
* ¼ cup water
* 5 cups sugar
* 2 oranges, seeded, finely chopped
* 1 lemon, seeded, finely chopped
* 1 cup raisins
* 1¼ teaspoons mace
* ¾ cups walnuts, roughly chopped
* 2 pouches (3 ounces each) liquid pectin

1. Wash the rhubarb, remove its leaves, and dice it.
2. Place the rhubarb and water in a large saucepan, bring to a boil, and simmer for 2 minutes.
3. Add the sugar, oranges, lemon, raisins, and mace, stirring until the sugar dissolves.
4. Bring the mixture to a rolling boil over medium-high heat. Stir in 2 pouches of liquid pectin. Return to a boil.
5. Boil hard for 1 minute, stirring constantly, and remove from heat.
6. Stir in the walnuts.
7. Ladle into prepared jars, leaving a ¼-inch headspace, and remove any bubbles.
8. Process the finished jars for 10 minutes.

Strawberry Lemon Marmalade

Yield: 7 half-pints

Ingredients:

* ¼ cup lemon peel, thinly sliced
* 1¾ quarts (approximately) strawberries, crushed to yield 4 cups
* 1 tablespoon lemon juice
* 6 cups sugar
* 1 box (1.75-ounce) dry pectin

1. Cover the lemon peel with water and boil for 5 minutes; drain.
2. Combine the cooked peel, strawberries, pectin, and lemon juice in a large saucepan; bring

slowly to a boil.

3. Add the sugar and stir until dissolved; bring to a rolling boil. Boil hard for 1 minute, stirring constantly.

4. Remove the saucepan from the heat and skim off the foam if necessary. Ladle into prepared jars, leaving a ¼-inch headspace.

5. Process the finished jars for 10 minutes.

Peach Preserves

Yield: 5 half-pints

Ingredients:

- ❧ 4 pounds (approximately) peaches, prepared to yield 4 cups
- ❧ 2 tablespoons lemon juice
- ❧ 7 cups sugar
- ❧ 1 box (1.75-ounce) dry pectin

1. If desired, blanch the peaches to slip off the skins (see "All About Blanching" in the appendix), then pit and slice the peaches.

2. Place the peaches, pectin, and lemon juice in a large saucepan. Bring to a boil, stirring gently.

3. Add the sugar all at once, stirring until dissolved. Return to a rolling boil and boil hard for 1 minute.

4. Remove the saucepan from heat and skim off the foam if necessary. Ladle into prepared jars, leaving a ¼-inch headspace, and remove any bubbles.

5. Process the finished jars for 20 minutes.

MAKING COOKED SOFT SPREADS WITHOUT ADDED PECTIN

Making cooked jams, jellies, and other soft spreads without added pectin will take a bit longer, use a bit less sugar, and require just a tad more judgment than making them with the added pectin, but the process is not difficult or daunting. Some folks claim that these soft spreads don't taste as fresh as those made with added pectin because they must be cooked longer, but honestly, we're just talking about degrees of delicious, not good versus bad. I've included a number of great recipes here, and you are sure to find others that you like.

Just minutes away from becoming a delcious strawberry jam! Don't forget to keep stirring as you boil the fruit to get your jam to the perfect consistency.

PROCESS OVERVIEW

1. Prepare your containers and water-bath canner.

2. Measure the sugar—about ¾ to 1 cup of sugar for each cup of juice or fruit—and set aside.

3. Prepare the fruit or juice, measuring precisely, and add lemon if necessary. When preparing fruit for jams, crush one layer of fruit at a time. If making jelly, cook the fruit and extract the juice (see "The Art of the Jelly Bag" in the appendix). For marmalades, conserves, and preserves, follow the directions for the texture of fruit.

4. Combine the fruit/juice and sugar in a saucepot until the sugar is dissolved. Add ½ teaspoon butter or margarine to reduce foaming if desired.

5. Bring the mixture quickly to a boil, and boil rapidly. As the mixture begins to thicken, stir frequently to prevent sticking or scorching.

6. Cook to the gelling point (see "Is It Jam Yet?" on page 127).

7. Remove from heat, skim off the foam, and ladle into prepared jars.

8. Now that you're ready to process the jars, see "Canning Soft Spreads" on page 149 for processing instructions.

Recipes for Soft Spreads without Pectin

For all recipes, after filling the jars to the required headspace, remove any bubbles, wipe the rims clean, adjust the lids, and process the jars for the stated time, adjusting as necessary for altitude (see "Altitude Adjustment" in the appendix).

JAMS

Apricot Jam

Yield: 9 half-pints

Ingredients:

❧ 8 pounds (approximately) apricots, prepared to yield 8 cups

❧ 4 tablespoons lemon juice

❧ 6 cups sugar

1. Peel, pit, and chop the apricots.

2. Follow the directions in the process overview under "Making Cooked Soft Spreads without Added Pectin" (opposite). Leave a 1/4-inch headspace. Process the finished jars for 10 minutes.

Berry Jam

This recipe works for blackberries, blueberries, raspberries, boysenberries, dewberries, gooseberries, loganberries, youngberries, and combinations of these fruits. Try different combinations—especially if you grow your own berries and don't have enough of one type. If you prefer seedless jam, heat the crushed berries until they're soft, press them through a sieve to remove the seeds, and measure out 9 cups of pulp for the recipe.

Yield: 6 half-pints

Ingredients:

❧ 4 1/2 quarts (approximately) berries, crushed to yield 9 cups

❧ 6 cups sugar

Follow the directions in the process overview under "Making Cooked Soft Spreads without Added Pectin" (opposite). Leave a 1/4-inch headspace. Process the finished jars for 15 minutes.

Strawberry Jam

Yield: 6 half-pints

Ingredients:

❖ 2 quarts strawberries, hulled and crushed

❖ 6 cups sugar

Follow the directions under "Making Cooked Soft Spreads without Added Pectin." Leave a ¼-inch headspace. Process the finished jars for 10 minutes.

JELLIES

Grape Jelly

Yield: 4 half-pints

Ingredients:

❖ 4 pounds grapes (dark blue varieties such as Concord, Wordon, or Fredonia)

❖ 3 cups sugar

1. Render the 4 pounds of grapes to achieve 4 cups of juice, following the instructions found in "The Art of the Jelly Bag" in the appendix.

2. After rendering the juice, let it sit for 12 hours to settle and then strain it through a coffee filter, ladling it carefully to avoid stirring sediment.

3. Continue with the directions under "Making Cooked Soft Spreads without Added Pectin." Leave a ¼-inch headspace. Process the finished jars for 10 minutes.

Mint Jelly

This is a great way to use your mint; this recipe makes a very nice garnish for lamb.

Yield: 4 half-pints

Ingredients:

❖ 1½ cups firmly packed spearmint leaves rendered to ½ cup extract

❖ 1 cup boiling water

❖ 4 pounds apples, prepared to yield 4 cups apple juice, or 4 cups commercially prepared apple juice.

❖ 2 tablespoons lemon juice

❖ 3 cups sugar

❖ Green food coloring (optional)

1. If preparing your own apple juice, follow the recipe on page 90 in chapter 4.

2. Place the mint leaves in a bowl, add boiling water, and let stand for at least 1 hour. Strain the leaves, squeezing them to extract the juice. Measure ½ cup of mint extract.

3. Place the apple juice, lemon juice, and mint extract in a large saucepan. Add the sugar all at once, stirring until it is dissolved. Bring to a boil over high heat, stirring constantly. Cook to the gelling point.

4. Remove from heat, skim off any foam, and ladle into prepared jars, leaving a ¼-inch headspace.

5. Process the finished jars for 10 minutes.

Spiced Apple Jelly

Yield: 4 half-pints

Ingredients:

❖ 4 pounds apples

❖ 3 cups sugar

❖ 2 tablespoons lemon juice

❖ 1 tablespoon whole cloves

❖ 1 tablespoon whole allspice

❖ 1 stick cinnamon

1. Tie the spices in a spice bag and cook with the apples to render 4 cups of apple juice, following the instructions found in "The Art of the Jelly Bag" in the appendix. Remove the spice bag before draining the juice to a measurement of 4 cups.

2. Continue with the directions under "Making Cooked Soft Spreads without Added Pectin." Leave a ¼-inch headspace. Process the finished jars for 10 minutes.

Blueberry Citrus Conserve

Yield: 4 half-pints

Ingredients:

- ❧ 2 cups water
- ❧ 4 cups sugar
- ❧ 1/3 cup thinly sliced lemon
- ❧ 1/2 cup thinly sliced orange
- ❧ 1/2 cup raisins
- ❧ 1 quart blueberries

1. Combine the water and sugar in a large saucepan. Bring to a boil and add the lemon, orange, and raisins. Simmer for 5 minutes. Add the blueberries. Stir, and cook rapidly almost to a gel state.

2. Remove from heat and skim off any foam. Ladle into prepared jars, leaving a 1/4-inch headspace, and remove any bubbles.

3. Process the finished jars for 15 minutes.

Cherry Marmalade

Yield: 4 half-pints

Ingredients:

- ❧ 4 cups sweet cherries, pitted
- ❧ 1 cup orange, seeded and finely chopped
- ❧ 3 1/2 cups sugar
- ❧ 4 tablespoons lemon juice

1. Combine all ingredients in a large saucepan and stir until the sugar dissolves.

2. Bring to a boil over high heat, stirring constantly. Cook rapidly almost to a gel state.

3. Remove from heat, skim off any foam, and ladle into prepared jars, leaving a 1/4-inch headspace.

4. Process the finished jars for 15 minutes.

Pear Preserves with Ginger

Yield: 7 half-pints

Ingredients:

❖ 5½ cups pears, peeled, cored, and finely chopped

❖ 3 limes, grated for zest, then juiced

❖ 2⅓ cups sugar

❖ 4 teaspoons fresh gingerroot, grated

1.   Combine pears, lime zest and juice, sugar, and gingerroot in a large saucepan. Bring to a boil over medium heat, stirring to dissolve the sugar.

2.   Boil, stirring frequently, until the mixture thickens and reaches a gel state.

3.   Remove from heat, skim off the foam, and ladle the preserves into prepared jars, leaving a ¼-inch headspace.

4.   Process the finished jars for 10 minutes.

Rich and satisfying flavors combined with smooth textures are the hallmark of great fruit butters.

MAKING FRUIT BUTTERS

Fruit butters, the most common and popular of which is apple butter, are a bit of a different species than the other soft spreads in that they rely on slow cooking to reduce the volume of water and achieve their smooth consistency. Other fruit spreads use rapid boiling to release the pectin and bind the water, sugar, and acid to form a gel. Unlike jams and chunky fruit spreads, most fruit-butter recipes encourage you to puree the fruit pulp. If you want, you can pull out some of your convenience appliances when you make fruit butters. One of the handiest is your slow cooker. Instead of cooking the pulp on your stovetop, you can use your slow cooker to reduce (but not eliminate) the need for watching and stirring the pulp.

PROCESS OVERVIEW

1.   Wash and prepare the fruit (blanch it if necessary [see "All About Blanching" in the appendix]; peel it; and remove cores, stems, seeds, pits, and blossom ends. Cut large fruit.).

2. Simmer the fruit with water or juice and spices, if called for, in a heavy stockpot, being careful not to scorch, until it becomes very soft.

3. Puree the cooked fruit in a mill or food processor to render the required amount of pulp.

4. Combine the pulp, sugar, and spices in the heavy stockpot, cooking slowly until it reaches the desired consistency and has the ability to mound up on a spoon (do not use conventional gel tests for fruit butters).

5. If the butter becomes too thick, add water or fruit juice to thin it.

6. Remove from heat and ladle into prepared jars, leaving the required headspace, and remove any air bubbles.

7. Now that you're ready to process the jars, see "Canning Soft Spreads" on page 149 for processing instructions.

Fruit Butter Recipes

Apricot Butter

Yield: 6 half-pints

Ingredients:

❦ 2 pounds or 24 medium apricots

❦ $\frac{1}{2}$ cup water

❦ $2\frac{1}{2}$ cups sugar

❦ 2 tablespoons lemon juice

1. Blanch washed apricots and then cool, peel, pit, and cut them in half.

2. Combine prepared apricots with $\frac{1}{2}$ cup of water to render $1\frac{1}{2}$ quarts of cooked apricot pulp.

3. Follow the directions for making fruit butters. Leave a $\frac{1}{4}$-inch headspace.

4. Process the finished jars for 10 minutes.

Crab Apple Butter

Yield: 6 half-pints

Ingredients:

❦ 4 pounds crab apples

❦ 1 cup water

❦ 2 cups sugar

❦ $1\frac{1}{2}$ teaspoons cinnamon

- ❖ ½ teaspoon cloves
- ❖ ½ to 1 teaspoon ginger, to taste

1. Combine washed and halved crab apples with 1 cup of water to prepare 6 cups of cooked crab apple pulp.
2. Follow the directions in the process overview under "Making Fruit Butters." Leave a ¼-inch headspace.
3. Process the finished jars for 10 minutes.

Peach Butter

Yield: 8 half-pints

Ingredients:

- ❖ 5 pounds or 18 to 20 medium peaches
- ❖ ½ cups water
- ❖ 3½ cups sugar

1. Blanch washed peaches and then cool, peel, pit, and cut them in half.
2. Combine prepared peaches with ½ cup of water to render 2 quarts of cooked apricot pulp.
3. Follow the directions in the process overview under "Making Fruit Butters." Leave a ¼-inch headspace.
4. Process the finished jars for 10 minutes.

Slow-Cooker Apple Butter

A word of warning: if you do an Internet search for apple-butter recipes, you'll find a ton of them out there, and many of them overlook such issues as what to do with the apple peels or invite you to store the butter without water-bath processing the jars. Many, *many* of them call for way more sugar than would suit even the sweetest tooth, and certainly more than is needed for preservation.

Here's a recipe that I like. This variety isn't quite as thick as that made by the conventional method, but it's an easy entrée into the world of fruit butters and pretty much makes itself.

Yield: 7 half-pints (depending upon consistency desired)

Ingredients:

- 10 to 12 large cooking apples, peeled, cored, and quartered (to make 14 cups)
- 2 cups white sugar
- $1/4$ cup apple juice
- $1/4$ cup apple cider vinegar
- 1 tablespoon ground cinnamon
- 1 whole cinnamon stick
- 1 to 2 teaspoons ground cloves (to taste)
- 1 to 2 teaspoons ground ginger (to taste)

1. Wash and drain the apples thoroughly and then peel, core, and quarter them. You should have 14 cups' worth. Place the apples in a slow cooker with the apple juice, vinegar, and sugar.

2. Cover and cook on low for 10 hours or overnight.

3. Remove the cover and, using a stick (immersion) blender, puree the apples until they are very smooth; alternately, you can put them into a blender or food processor and blend on high speed until smooth.

4. Return the pureed apples to the slow cooker, add the cinnamon stick, and cook uncovered until they are almost the desired consistency. Depending upon the water content of your apples, this could be another 1 to 6 hours.

5. Add the spices, stir, and cook for another hour. Taste the result and add more spices if desired.

6. Continue to cook on low until the mixture reaches the desired consistency.

7. Fill warm Mason jars to a $1/4$-inch headspace and seal each with a two-piece lid.

8. Process the finished jars in a water-bath canner: 10 minutes for half-pints or 15 minutes for pints.

CANNING EQUIPMENT RECAP

Here's a quick list of what you need for water-bath canning. Check out chapter 4 for detailed information.

❖ Water-bath canner with rack
❖ Mason jars: half-pint, pint, or 12-ounce jelly jars are often preferred
❖ Lids and screw bands
❖ Canning funnel
❖ Jar lifter
❖ Lid lifter
❖ Bubble probe (for chunky spreads)
❖ Clean cloths

CANNING SOFT SPREADS

Following is an overview of water-bath canning; for detailed instructions, see chapter 4.

1. Prepare the jars, lids, and bands. Keep both the jars and the lids warm.
2. Prepare the water-bath canner, bringing the water to a simmer (not a boil) prior to placing jars in the bath.
3. Clean the fruit thoroughly; cut out any bad spots; prepare it according to your recipe. Make the soft spread according to your recipe, skimming off foam as necessary. Taking one jar at a time, fill

the hot jar with hot syrup, leaving the required headspace. Remove any bubbles.
4. Wipe the rim of the jar using a clean, damp cloth and then place the rim on the lid and screw on the band.
5. Place the finished jars in the water-bath canner as they are filled and lidded.

6

6. When the canner is full, make sure that the jars are covered with 1 to 2 inches of water. Place the lid on the canner, bring the water to a boil, and continue to boil gently for the required processing time, adjusting as necessary for altitude (see "Altitude Adjustment" in the appendix). Don't start timing until the water has started to boil.

7. After the processing time is complete, turn off the stovetop's heat, remove the lid from the canner, and wait 5 minutes.

8. Use the jar lifter to remove the jars from the canner and place them on a rack or a layer of towels, away from drafts. Do not tighten or touch the bands. Allow the jars to cool for 12 to 24 hours.

9. Test the seal (lids should be concave, not convex, and should ping when tapped). When you're sure that the jars are sealed, remove the bands, label and date the jars, and store your homemade soft spread for up to one year.

9

IF IT DOESN'T LOOK JUST LIKE THE PICTURE...

It doesn't happen often, but sometimes your soft spread doesn't look like the pictures in this book or other recipe sources you find. Generally, if you follow the directions, precisely measure the proportions of the ingredients, prepare your jars and lids properly, and process the jars for the correct length of time, you won't have problems. The high acid and sugar content of fruit soft spreads makes them very easy to preserve safely. In most cases, problems involve cosmetic and consistency issues rather than safety or food-poisoning concerns. For example, I once made my favorite red-raspberry jam but was chatting with my husband and put the pectin in at the wrong time. The result was red-raspberry sauce, not jam. It was delicious, but very runny—actually perfect for ice cream, but not so great on toast. Other, more serious issues, such as mold, are usually quite obvious.

Before you put the jars away, check them to be sure that they have all sealed. Tap the lid and you'll get a high-pitched *ping*. When you look at the lids, they will be concave, not convex. If the jars haven't sealed, either store them in the refrigerator and use them quickly or remake them as described in "Remaking Jams and Jellies" on page 152.

PROBLEMS AND SOLUTIONS

Here are some of the common problems and what likely caused them:

❖ **Too soft**. Perhaps your proportions were wrong, you made too big of a batch, you didn't boil the fruit long enough, the fruit was too ripe, or—if this is a spread to which you added pectin—you added the wrong kind or not enough. When selecting your fruit, always add a small amount (say, 10 percent) of slightly underripe (not unripe) fruit. Another reminder—don't do double batches. Anything more than 5 to 6 cups of fruit or juice is probably too much. Remember, too, that the type of pectin that you add is not interchangeable. Read and follow the instructions that came with your pectin. If you're not using pectin, check the calibration on your candy thermometer and/or use either the cold-plate or sheeting test (see "Is It Jam Yet? on page 127) to confirm the gel. You may want to consider remaking the jam (see "Remaking Jams and Jellies" on page 152).

❖ **Too stiff**. Maybe you added too much sugar, boiled the fruit for too long, or added too much pectin (either natural or commercial). If your recipe requires you to add pectin, follow the recipe proportions and timing carefully. If you're not using pectin, check the calibration on your candy thermometer and/or use either the cold-plate or sheeting test to confirm the gel. While many recipes differ, if you're making a recipe without added pectin, generally $^3/_4$ to 1 cup of sugar per cup of fruit or juice is reasonable.

❖ **Cloudy**. There are a number of possible causes here, one of which is cooking the fruit too long before straining, causing small particles to break off into the juice. Using green fruit or allowing the hot syrup to cool before ladling it into jars will also affect the clarity. The biggest culprit may be your jelly bag (if it's old, it may have allowed particles through) or that you tried to rush the juice out of the bag by squeezing.

❧ **Sugar crystals or weepy fluids.** Neither of these conditions is serious. Crystals may be caused by using too much sugar or not cooking properly (too slowly, too long, or not long enough). Sometimes undissolved sugar crystals clinging to the side of the saucepot will accidentally fall into the jar when you're ladling the syrup. Weeping and seeping (called syneresis) is usually caused by the quantity of acid and quality of the pectin in the fruit, but this can also be caused by less-than-ideal storage conditions. If caused by the natural acid and pectin in the fruit, there's not much to be done. Before you serve your spread, simply mop up the extra liquid using a clean paper towel. Always store canned foods in a cool, dry, dark location.

❧ **Crystals in grape jelly.** This could be tartaric acid, a normal (and harmless) component of grapes. To reduce the possibility of tartaric-acid crystals, let the grape juice sit overnight in the refrigerator before making your jelly. Ladle the juice from the top, being careful not to disturb the particles that have settled on the bottom, and strain the juice through a damp jelly bag.

❧ **Bubbling/fermentation.** If there are active bubbles in the jar—in other words, the bubbles are moving when the jar is still—then your spread is fermenting, and that's not good. This was probably caused by failure to bring the syrup to a full, rolling boil and to reach 220 degrees Fahrenheit, the temperature required to kill all microorganisms in the syrup. Other possibilities include the jars not being cleaned properly or not being processed long enough in the water bath.

❧ **Mold**. Don't use the spread if there's mold on the top. Sorry Mom—I know you told us just to scrape it off. But moms are not always right. Mold can be caused by all of the reasons in the preceding bullet point along with too much headspace. If you don't fill your jars according to directions and leave too much distance between the jam and the lid, the physics at work here won't allow a tight enough vacuum to form. Without that nice tight seal, unfriendly microorganisms can sneak in and set up house.

REMAKING JAMS AND JELLIES

If your spread is too soft, you may wish to remake it. If it's only slightly soft, especially if it's a jam, it may be just fine. If you made the jam or jelly using commercial pectin, follow the remake instructions on the package. If you made it without pectin, work in batches of no more than 4 cups of jam or jelly at a time. Bring the jam/jelly to a full boil, and boil for 2 minutes. Test for gel using the candy thermometer, sheeting, or cold-plate method (see "Is It Jam Yet?" on page 127). When it's reached the proper temperature or consistency, remove the jam/jelly from the heat, skim off any foam, and ladle into hot jars, again leaving the appropriate headspace. Wipe the jars' lids clean, adjust the two-piece caps, and process the jars for the full time in the water-bath canner.

LABELING AND STORAGE

The jars are lined up neatly on the counter and have cooled. You've waited the necessary twenty-four hours and have checked that all of the lids are sealed and the spreads have set properly. What a pretty sight! As with other canned goods, remove the band, wipe the jar to remove any food

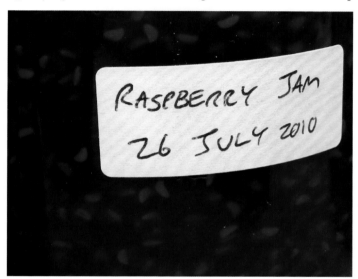

particles, and attach a label with the contents, date, and batch (if necessary). Add these jars to your canning inventory, and then store them in a cool, dry place—that's if you can resist the urge to enjoy some right away! See "Store and Enjoy" in chapter 4 for details about the canning inventory and optimal storage conditions.

FUN AND FANCY WRAPPING

Some manufacturers make lovely (and somewhat pricey) jars with decorative embossing and other graphic accents. These fancy jars and lids make beautiful gifts. You can also find very stylish jar labels—even some that are personalized. While none of this is really necessary for adequate preservation, it sure does make gift-giving easy. If you compare the cost of these high-end jars and labels (and the cost of the ingredients) with the cost of other gifts and gift wrapping, you might find that your homemade jam is not only delicious, but it's also a bargain, and the size is always right!

CHAPTER 6

Pickles, Relishes, Salsas, and Such

Can you eat a deli sandwich without that half-sour spear next to it? Of course you can, but the meal is so much better with it! The pickle, the sweet relish, the ketchup, the spicy mustard, the tangy salsa, the "sour" kraut (sauerkraut)—they all add a dimension of flavor and texture to our meals that would be missing if our ancestors hadn't figured out these clever ways to preserve cucumbers, cabbage, peppers, and other summer vegetables.

When folks start to talk about pickles, relishes, chutneys, salsas, sauerkraut, brines, fermentation, and more, it's easy to get overwhelmed and feel that these types of preserved foods are just too difficult to make yourself. As you'll soon see, that's simply not true. We've built on what our ancestors devised out of necessity and have developed ways of preparing and preserving classic pickled foods in ways that are less complicated and take less time, yet deliver great flavor. In this chapter, we'll cover both the old- and the new-fashioned methods, culling the huge ocean of pickling possibilities to give you great recipes to start (or continue) your pickling career. We'll begin by exploring the types of pickled foods, how one type of preservation is different from another, and what kind of ingredients and equipment you'll need. We'll then walk step-by-step through some of the basic recipes involving pickled and fermented food.

Unless you plan to eat your pickles, relish, and such right away, you'll want to preserve them. You'll do this with your water-bath canner, a tool you've become very familiar with by now (but you'll find a refresher at the end of the chapter).

Savor summer all year long with the brisk flavor of sweet relish.

IT'S NOT JUST ABOUT PICKLES ANYMORE!

Sure, you want to make a great pickle. It's a primal food preservation challenge that ranks right up there with sauerkraut. But if you set your sights just on the obvious, you're going to miss some great mealtime additions. Here are the types of pickled products that we'll cover in this chapter:

❖ **Pickles.** I include both old-fashioned brined (fermented) pickles and new-fashioned fresh-pack pickles. There are even refrigerator pickles that require no processing. When most people hear the word "pickle," they think of cucumbers, but other delicious possibilities abound with other vegetables and fruit.

❖ **Relishes.** These are made from ground or chopped vegetables that are cooked in a tangy vinegar syrup with spices. People often think of red or green hotdog relish, but there are many other options!

❖ **Salsas.** Salsas are a close cousin to relishes and are generally a mixture of chopped fruits and vegetables cooked with vinegar or lemon juice and a variety of herbs and spices. Originally associated with ethnic foods, salsas are considered by some to be today's condiment of choice.

❖ **Chutneys and Sauces.** These are also part of the relish/salsa family tree. Chutneys distinguish themselves as chunkier combinations of fruits and vegetables with strong, spicy flavors that are developed from long cooking times. Sauces ranging from mild to hot are likewise simmered for long periods to achieve the desired flavor and consistency. Sauces are probably on the outer fringes of the family in terms of their appearance, but their ingredients are consistent with the others.

Sweet cranberry chutney is a welcome addition to any meal, whether it's the Thanksgiving feast or just "porkchop Wednesday."

BRINE, FERMENTATION, AND OTHER PICKLE TERMS

We will try to cut through much of the technical jargon associated with pickling and leave you empowered rather than intimidated. Think back to the "good old days" and picture an old-fashioned general store with a big barrel of pickles by the counter—those pickles were most likely brined and fermented. They probably took a month or more to reach their tangy flavor and, more importantly, created the chemistry that preserved them while they sat in the barrel unrefrigerated.

In the first couple of chapters of this book, we discussed how acid levels help to protect fruits and vegetables from spoilage. The pickling process is about making sure that there's enough acid to prevent the growth of food-spoiling microorganisms and thus preserve the vegetable or fruit. You can do that in one of two primary ways: by brining/fermenting, which creates lactic acid, or by adding acid, usually through vinegar. There are a number of variations of each of these methods, but they all come down to either *creating* or *adding* an acid. We'll group our recipes into these two primary categories: *fermented* and *unfermented* (called "fresh pack") pickle products.

FERMENTED PICKLED PRODUCTS

Brine is typically a mixture of salt and water. When you put a vegetable into a brine, the salt will draw the moisture and sugars out of the vegetable. If then left in the right conditions, a bit of chemistry takes place and lactic acid bacteria (harmless microbes that are naturally present on the surface of vegetables) grow because they like the salty environment. In gratitude for you having provided such happy conditions, these bacteria produce lactic acid, a preservative. Other, less benign microbes can't flourish in the salty and increasingly acidic environment. This is called lactic fermentation. You'll know that your cucumbers are fermenting because the

Fermented pickles only require salt and water for preservation, but dill, garlic, and other herbs and spices add interest and tang to your dills.

liquid will start to bubble. When the fermentation is complete, the bubbling stops. The cucumber now has a different taste and texture, and the pH level has dropped to a safe acidity. In short, the cucumber has turned into a pickle. You can then add spices and other ingredients and process the cucumbers to create a particular style of pickle, and the lactic fermentation that created the acid will help preserve it. According to the United States Department of Agriculture (USDA), you can store *fermented pickles* in their crock for up to six months, but the preferred method for long-term storage is processing in a water-bath canner. For long-term preservation *of all other fermented products*, you must process them in a water-bath canner.

Have friends over on Saturday night and plan your meal around your homemade chutney. It's sure to be a hit.

UNFERMENTED PICKLED PRODUCTS

In these types of recipes, the vegetables and fruits will not ferment. Included here are a wide variety of tasty, interesting, and easy-to-prepare foods, such as fresh-pack pickles, refrigerator pickles, relishes, salsas, chutneys, and fruit pickles. Some of these foods may soak in a brine for just a short time, from a few hours to a few days—long enough to draw out some of the moisture and sugar, but not long enough to start fermentation. But for many, there is no brine at all. To achieve the acidity needed, the recipe will call for adding an acid—usually vinegar but sometimes lemon juice—to the pickling solution or sauce. For long-term storage, you'll process the finished jars in a water-bath canner.

You'll only need a handful of ingredients for making pickles, and they are all easily found at your local grocery store.

THE ESSENTIALS

The food that we've included in the pickled-product family all carry a consistent "DNA" developed by the types of ingredients that go into their recipes. They contain the following ingredients in one form or another.

Scour your neighborhood for places to find farm-fresh produce. Farmer's markets are always a good bet, but see if you have any Community Supported Agriculture nearby, too.

PRODUCE

Fresh, fresh, fresh is best, best, best! I can't repeat that often enough. As with other home food preservation, look for local fruits and vegetables at the peak of perfection. Check the recipe, though; it's better for some fruit pickles to be slightly under ripe. For all fruits and vegetables, refrigerate them until you are ready to use them, then wash them thoroughly. If you notice cucumbers floating to the top of the water during washing, do not use them for whole pickles; they have hollow centers. Use these for a relish instead.

Cucumbers are particularly demanding when it comes to pickling suitability. First, look for varieties described as pickling. The sign at the farm stand or grocery will state that clearly. If you grow your own, your seed catalog should have a section of pickling cukes. Some varieties of pickling cucumbers include Kirby, Bush Pickle, Carolina, and the West Indian Gherkin (the ideal pickling gherkin). You won't get a good pickle from a salad cuke. And don't use waxed cucumbers! The coating will prevent the brine and pickling syrup from penetrating. This shouldn't be a problem if you are growing your own cucumbers or getting them from a local farm. Consider the size relative to the recipe. The 1½-inch cukes work well for gherkins while the larger, 4-inch cukes work well for dills. Use the more mature or odd-shaped cukes for relishes or pickle mixes where the shape and the soft, seedy center isn't a concern. Pickle your cukes the day they're picked, or your results will be sad and soft. *Note: You should always trim ¹⁄₁₆ inch off the blossom end of the cucumber to remove enzymes that can cause softening.*

Choose cucumbers that are freshly picked and not overly developed. The larger cucumbers will have soft centers and big seeds.

SALT

Salt is a utility player when it comes to pickling. It functions as both a flavoring and a preservative, and it helps the crispness of the pickle. Whether it's in a brine or just as an ingredient in your pickle product, choose your salt carefully. *Note: use only canning or pickling salt—not table salt.* Table salt is blended with iodine and additives to prevent caking. These additives can cause your pickles to be dark and the brine cloudy.

If you are on a salt-restricted diet, fermented foods can be a problem because of the high sodium content. Do not reduce the salt in the brine of a fermented pickle or sauerkraut. The good news is that the USDA has developed lower-sodium pickle recipes using a fresh-pack process.

If you want your pickles to be bright and flavorful, use only pickling and/or canning salt, which is specially formulated for this purpose.

SPICES AND HERBS

They're not the biggest ingredients in your pickle product, but spices and herbs are important. Most of the recipes in this chapter call for various spices. You won't need very much of any one of them for most recipes, maybe a teaspoon or tablespoon or two. Unless you've tried the recipe before, use the amounts suggested. Many of the spices used are quite potent, and changes in the amounts will have a significant effect on the outcome. Unless the recipe states

You can find premixed pickling spices in your local grocery store, buy a commercial mix, or make your own if you wish. Just make sure the spices you use are fresh.

differently, use whole spices. Many recipes call for pickling spice, which is a combination of a number of spices. American varieties include coriander, mustard seed, cloves, cinnamon, ginger, bay leaves, and black pepper. Indian pickling spices often also use turmeric, cardamom, and chili peppers. If you don't find pickling spice at your local grocery store, it's readily available via mail order (see Resources), or if you use a lot, you might want to make your own custom blend.

THE SPICE OF LIFE

It's easy to think of those little tins as permanent fixtures on your spice rack, but check their expiration dates. (Many spice manufacturers have websites that allow you to check the expiration code.) Although spices can be pretty expensive—some of those little tins can cost close to ten dollars—it's worth replacing any that have expired. Spices *do* lose their flavor. Don't invest your time, talent, and fresh produce in a relish and then leave it tasting flat because the spices were old.

VINEGAR

Vinegar, like salt, is a multitasker. It maintains a safe acid level, thereby preserving the food, and it adds that zest that we associate with the pickle family. Be choosy with your vinegar; read the labels. Most recipes call for high-grade cider or white distilled vinegar that is at least 5 percent acidity. This is very important. Using a vinegar with a lower level of acidity can jeopardize the safety of your food. If the bottle does not display the acidity percentage, don't use that vinegar. Always follow the proportions in the recipe exactly. Adding less vinegar or diluting it will reduce the overall acidity and—again—jeopardize the safety of your food.

Read the label before you buy vinegar for your pickling project. Make sure that it's at least 5 percent acidic.

Let the recipe guide you in your choice of cider versus white vinegar. If the recipe doesn't specify, then you can choose between the two. Consider that cider vinegar tends to be less pungent but may darken your pickle. The opposite is true for white vinegar: truer color, sharper flavor.

SWEETENERS

Let the recipe guide you here, as well. Recipes generally call for granulated white cane or beet sugar. Occasionally, you'll find one that uses brown sugar, honey, or even maple syrup. The

Once you have all of your ingredients ready, you'll combine them to make your pickling syrup, which will give your pickles that flavor you've grown to know and love.

latter will produce a slightly darker product. Do not substitute artificial sweeteners or the newer plant-based sweeteners unless you find a tested recipe. The chemistry needed to preserve the pickles doesn't work the same with these sweetening products.

WATER

Using water should be simple, but it might not be, depending on where you live. Good pickle products need water that isn't heavy in calcium and minerals (hard water), or they risk turning dark or shriveling. If you don't have naturally soft water, plan to use distilled water, which is inexpensive and readily available in most grocery stores.

FIRMING AGENTS

Some recipes call for firming agents such as alum, limewater solutions, or food-grade calcium chloride. The US Department of Agriculture does not include firming agents in their recipes. They feel that if you use very fresh ingredients—especially cucumbers not older than twenty-four hours—you should have no trouble with soft pickles. It comes down to a matter of preference. Alum and food-grade lime (known as pickling lime) is safe to use as long you follow the directions. One well-known brand is Mrs. Wages Pickling Lime. I found that my sweet pickles, which seemed very soft when I put them into the jars, "crisped up" nicely after they were processed and stored for a few weeks, while my dills do benefit from the pickling lime.

EQUIPMENT

Other than perhaps a crock for fermented pickles or sauerkraut, you probably have most of the equipment that you'll need to make the pickled products we'll cover here. If you're planning to preserve your pickled products for later use, you'll need water-bath canning equipment and jars (see chapter 4). All equipment must be resistant to interaction with the acid and the salt. Do not use any galvanized, aluminum, brass, copper, or iron containers for fermenting pickles or sauerkraut. Beyond the canning equipment, here's what you need:

❖ A large pot or crock (for brining fermented vegetables as in long-brine pickles and sauerkraut) made of stoneware, unchipped enamel, glass, or food-grade plastic that is deep enough to allow room for the vegetables to be covered completely with 1 to 2 inches of brine—held submerged below the brine by a lid or plate and weights to hold it down—plus a few inches of headspace above the lid (if the crock is fitted with a lid, the lid must be undersized to allow for expansion from moisture)

❖ A large (8- to 10-quart) pot made of unchipped enamel, stainless steel, or glass for heating pickling liquids for pickled products that are not fermented

❖ Large bowls and shallow pans for collecting and staging produce

❖ A colander, knives, a vegetable peeler, and a cutting board for washing and preparing produce

❖ A food scale, food grinder for relishes and blender or immersion blender for sauces

❖ Utensils and incidentals such as long-handled ladles and spoons, clean cloths and towels, oven mitts, a timer or clock, and measuring cups or 1- or 2-quart measuring pitchers (avoid wooden spoons)

❖ A spice bag or cheesecloth for seasoning in some recipes

❖ A mandolin food slicer is a nice-to-have (but optional) item for thinly slicing vegetables, such as the cabbage for sauerkraut or beautifully sliced pickles

Pickling requires much of the same equipment in pickling that you've been using for canning and jamming.

USE KEEPSAKE CROCKS FOR DECORATION

For long-brine, fermented pickles and sauerkraut, make sure that the crock you use is squeaky clean and in perfect condition, free from hairline cracks and nicks. As charming as the thought of using Grandma's old crock might be, it's probably better to use it as a doorstop. Those almost-invisible cracks can provide refuge for microorganisms that can ruin your pickling project. When you're ready to use a crock, whether old or new, be sure to scrub it thoroughly to remove any trace of food particles or invisible food film. They, too, can cause pickling failure.

WHERE AND HOW TO BEGIN

If you've turned to this section of the book, you probably have a good idea of what you'd like to make—pickles, relish, salsa, and so on. However, if you're new at this and not really sure what you have the courage to try first, here's a suggestion: Relishes and salsas are less demanding in terms of time, and more forgiving in terms of the ingredients. If you don't have ready access to vine-fresh pickling cucumbers, you can make many great relishes or salsas using ingredients that are very common, such as corn, cabbage, onions, and peppers. If you want to be really simple—and there's nothing wrong with simple—you can find premixed kits for dill and bread-and-butter pickles, as well as for tomato salsa (see Resources).

With their combination of festive colors, these jars of pickles and relish make great holiday gifts. Just add a ribbon and a label, and you're done!

Next, consider fresh-pack (short-brine) pickles, then chutneys and sauces, and lastly fermented (long-brine) pickles and sauerkraut. You can make many types of fresh-pack pickles in one day, though some will ask for an overnight brine soak. I put fermented pickles and sauerkraut last because they require a fairly long time commitment (daily babysitting or, in other words, a quick check, for up to six weeks), and they are less tolerant of less-than-fresh produce. The initial preparation is not difficult, but you do need to be very selective with the equipment and diligent about caring for the pickles during the fermentation period.

Whichever product you decide to try, start by reviewing the recipe carefully and making sure that you have all of the ingredients and equipment that you need before you begin.

Pickling Dos and Don'ts

✤ Measure ingredients accurately, using the exact amounts of vegetables, fruit, salt, and vinegar that are called for.

✤ If brining, follow the exact proportions for the water and salt given in the recipe. It can be tempting to reduce the salt, but the proportions are crucial for inducing the fermentation and formation of acid.

✤ For fresh-pack, or short-brine, pickled products, wait four to six weeks before enjoying. This gives the produce time to absorb the spices and flavors. It's not necessary to wait for fermented products because, once the fermenting is finished, they have already had plenty of time to develop their distinctive flavors.

✤ For fermented products, do not allow a scum to form on the top of the brine. During the course of the brining period, check the crock every day or so and remove any scum. This scum can reduce the acidity of the brine and compromise its ability to preserve the vegetable.

✤ When cleaning the vegetables, especially cucumbers, scrub them well using a vegetable brush under cold running water to remove any soil that might try to cling to the dimply skin. If the recipe calls for peeling the vegetable, wash it whole before peeling. Cut off $1/16$ inch from the blossom end. Unless the recipe calls for it, you do not need to cut off the stem end.

✤ When working with hot peppers, or even some varieties of red bell peppers, wear rubber gloves to protect your skin from burns.

✤ If pickling green mangoes, use caution because this fruit belongs to the same family as poison ivy. Some people react to mangoes in the same fashion as they would poison ivy.

LET'S DO IT!

You've got your equipment, your produce, and your vision of beautifully canned pickles or relishes—now let's roll up our sleeves and get to work. The first section will cover fresh-pack products; the second covers fermented products.

MAKING UNFERMENTED (FRESH-PACK) PICKLE PRODUCTS

I've divided this part into two sections. First is an overview of how to make fresh-pack pickles. Then you'll find recipes with the specific ingredients, preparation instructions, and canning details.

PACKING WHOLE PICKLES

If you're making whole pickles, such as full-size dills, here are two tips to make your life easier:

❖ Use wide-mouthed Mason jars—these are much easier to fill with large produce.

❖ Pack whole pickles first; then fill the spaces with halves or spears (they will slide in nicely if you gently push them in against the side of the jar).

PROCESS OVERVIEW

Most fresh-pack pickles follow these basic steps. Some will require a short-brine or salting. Some recipes call for raw-packing, while others call for hot-packing. Check your recipe for specific details.

1. Prepare your jars and water-bath canner.
2. Prepare the brine if one is called for in the recipe.

Making the Brine

A brine is simply water saturated with salt. A standard salt brine is a 10 percent solution of water and salt. To make this, combine and dissolve $\frac{1}{2}$ cup of canning or pickling salt for each quart of water. Be sure to use soft water, or use distilled water if your water is naturally hard. Always check your recipe. Many recipes for fermented pickles call for brine with vinegar, in addition to the salt.

3. Thoroughly wash all vegetables, cutting $\frac{1}{16}$ inch off the blossom end. Cut, slice, chop, or grind the vegetables as directed in the recipe.

4. Brine or salt your vegetables if necessary, then rinse them thoroughly and drain them completely. Set them aside.

5. Prepare a spice bag if it's called for in the recipe.

6. If making raw-pack pickles, pack them cold in a hot jar. Pack whole pickles first, then add spears to fill the spaces.

7. Combine your vinegar or lemon with the other ingredients in a large stainless-steel or enamel pot, and bring it to a boil to form the pickling syrup.

• If making raw-pack pickles, pour the pickling syrup over the pickles.

• If making hot-pack pickled products, add the vegetables to the hot pickling syrup, heat or cook the combination according

to the directions, remove the pot from the heat, and pack the hot produce into hot jars with the syrup.

8. Remove any bubbles, adjust the two-piece caps, and process the finished jars. See "Canning Pickled Products" on page 188.

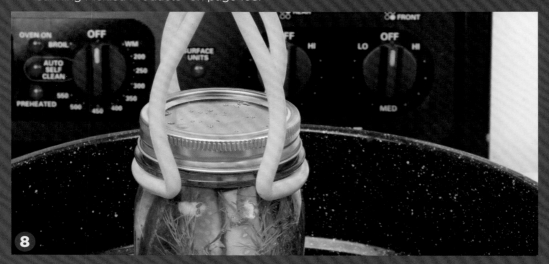

Salting Vegetables

Some recipes, most often those for fresh-pack pickles or relishes, call for salting the vegetables before pickling them. This salting helps to draw out the juices from the vegetable, making the finished product crisper. The process is simple. Put the prepared and drained vegetables in a suitably sized container (food-grade plastic, stainless steel, aluminum, or unchipped enamel). The container should be more than twice the volume of the prepared vegetables. Sprinkle the salt on top of the vegetables, and pat them down. Some recipes call for covering the vegetables with ice cubes. Let the vegetables sit for the length of time called for in the recipe, then thoroughly rinse off all the salt. *This step is very important.* If you leave too much salt, it will affect the flavor of your finished pickled product.

To thoroughly rinse the salted vegetables, fill the container with cold, fresh water and gently stir to mix and cleanse the vegetables. Drain off the salted water. Repeat this at least one more time or until you have removed all of the salt. Pour the vegetables into a large colander to drain them thoroughly before using them in your recipe. If you have salted ground vegetables, you may need to line the colander with several layers of cheesecloth. Squeeze the cheesecloth to ring out excess liquid.

Fresh-Pack Pickle, Relish, and Salsa Recipes

In all of these recipes, be sure to use nonreactive pots, pans, bowls, and implements (stainless steel, glass, enamel, or food-grade plastic), as well as 5 percent acid vinegar. For each jar, allow the required headspace; wipe the rim clean; adjust the cap; and process the jar for the amount of time stated.

PICKLES

Kosher Dill Pickles

Yield: 4 quarts or 8 pints

Ingredients:

- 7 pounds pickling cucumbers
- 6 cups water
- 2½ cups white vinegar (5% acidity)
- 1 package Ball Simple Creations Kosher Dill Pickle Mix

1. Thoroughly wash the cucumbers. Cut off $\frac{1}{16}$ inch from blossom end and cut the cucumber into spears.
2. Pack the cucumbers into the jars, leaving a ½-inch headspace.
3. Ladle the pickling syrup over the cucumbers, leaving the same ½-inch headspace.
4. Process the finished jars in a water-bath canner: 15 minutes for both pints and quarts.

Sharon and Carol's Not-Too-Hot Dill Pickles

Yield: 6 quarts or 12 pints

Ingredients:

- 10 pounds pickling cucumbers
- 2 quarts water
- 1½ quarts cider vinegar (5% acidity)
- 1⅓ cups pickling or canning salt
- For each jar: 1 hot pepper, 1 teaspoon dill seed or 1 head dill weed, 1½ teaspoon pickling spices, and 2 individual cloves garlic

1. Thoroughly wash the cucumbers. Cut off $\frac{1}{16}$ inch from blossom end, and cut the cucumbers into spears or leave them whole.

2. Place the cucumbers in a large, nonreactive container (glass, stainless steel, crockery, plastic) and cover with a solution of 1 cup of pickling salt for each gallon of water.

3. Place a plate on top of the pickles to keep them submerged; soak overnight.

4. Drain off the salt-water solution and thoroughly rinse the cucumbers, then drain them.

5. Mix the water, vinegar, and remaining salt in a medium saucepan, and heat to a boil to make the pickling syrup.

6. In each hot jar, place the hot pepper, dill, pickling spice, and garlic. Pack the cucumbers on top, leaving a $\frac{1}{2}$-inch headspace.

7. Ladle the pickling syrup over the cucumbers, leaving the same $\frac{1}{2}$-inch headspace.

8. Process the finished jars: 15 minutes for both pints and quarts.

Sweet Sandwich Pickles

These are the perfect size, shape, and flavor! They're a big hit with the men in my family.

Yield: 6 pints

Ingredients:

- 4 pounds pickling cucumbers
- 1 cup pickling or canning salt
- 24 cups water (divided)
- 10 cups white vinegar (5% acidity)
- 2 cups brown sugar, lightly packed
- 2 cups white granulated sugar
- 2 teaspoons celery seed
- 2 teaspoons mustard seed
- 1 teaspoon ground turmeric

1. Wash and trim the cucumbers, then slice them lengthwise in $\frac{1}{4}$-inch-thick slices. Place the cut cucumbers in a glass, stainless, or enamel container.

2. Combine the pickling salt with 16 cups of water in a large container. Stir until the salt dissolves. Pour this over the cucumbers, covering them completely. Put a plate on the cukes to keep them submerged. Let these stand in a cool place (70 to 75°F) for 3 hours. Rinse the cukes thoroughly under cool, running water and then drain them.

3. Combine 6 cups of vinegar and 6 cups of water in a large pan and bring it to a boil. Add the drained cucumber slices and return to a boil, cooking gently until

heated through but not soft, about 5 minutes. Drain well, discarding the liquid.

4. In a large pot, combine the remaining 4 cups of vinegar, 2 cups of water, brown and white sugars, and spices. Bring to a boil, stirring to dissolve the sugar, and cook the resulting syrup for 10 minutes. Add the drained cucumbers and return quickly just to a boil, then remove the pot from the heat.

5. Pack the hot cucumber slices into hot jars, leaving a 1/2-inch headspace. Add the hot pickling syrup, leaving the same 1/2-inch headspace.

6. Process the finished pints for 15 minutes.

Helen's Watermelon Rind Pickles

My mom used to make these when I was a child, and I thought they were weird. Now, they're considered gourmet, trendy, and very sustainable.

Yield: 5 pints

Ingredients:

✤ 16 cups watermelon rind in 1-inch cubes (trim away all of the pink flesh and green skin)

✤ 1 cup pickling salt

✤ 2 gallons water, divided

✤ 3 sticks cinnamon

✤ 1 tablespoon whole cloves

✤ 1/2 teaspoon ground ginger

✤ 1 tablespoon whole allspice

✤ 1/2 teaspoon mustard seed

✤ 7 cups sugar

✤ 1 medium lemon, thinly sliced

✤ 2 cups white vinegar

1. Mix the salt and 1 gallon of water together, pour over the rind, cover, and let sit overnight.

2. Drain and rinse the rind thoroughly.

3. Place the rind in a large saucepan, cover with 1 gallon of water, bring to a boil, and simmer until tender, about 10 minutes. Drain the rind and set it aside.

4. Tie the spices in a spice bag. Combine the spice bag, sugar, lemon, and vinegar in a large saucepan; bring the mixture to a boil; and simmer it for 10 minutes.

5. Add the rind and simmer until it is transparent and the liquid has thickened slightly (about 45 minutes). Remove the spice bag.

6. Pack the hot rind and syrup into hot jars, leaving a 1/2-inch headspace.

7. Process the finished pints for 10 minutes.

Season's End Mixed-Vegetable Pickles

This is a great and easy way to use "this" and "that" at the end of the growing season. These pickles look great next to your favorite sandwich, and they're tangy and tasty, too.

Yield: 5 pints

Ingredients:

* 1 pound zucchini, cut into ¼-inch slices
* 1 pound green beans, whole with ends trimmed
* ½ pound carrots, cut into ¼-inch slices
* ¾ pound pearl onions, peeled and trimmed
* 2 large red and 2 large green bell peppers; stems, blossoms, and membranes removed; then cut into ½-inch vertical slices
* 1 cup light brown sugar
* 1 cup white sugar
* 2 tablespoons dry mustard
* 2 tablespoons whole mustard seed
* 1½ tablespoons canning salt
* 1 teaspoon ground cinnamon
* 1 teaspoon ground ginger
* 3 cups cider vinegar

1. Cut, wash, drain, and mix the vegetables; set them aside.
2. Combine the remaining ingredients in a large saucepan, and bring the mixture to a boil. Add the vegetables and return to a boil, then simmer for 10 minutes.
3. Pack the hot vegetables and syrup into hot jars, leaving a ¼-inch headspace.
4. Process the finished pints for 15 minutes.

Aunt Suzy's Sweet Holiday Relish

This is the best—absolutely *the best*—relish you'll ever taste. Making it is a two-day project: you grind and salt the vegetables on day one, let them sit overnight, and then can them the next day. It is well worth the effort! I'm forever indebted to my sister, Suzy, who gave me this recipe many years ago. If you can't find red bell peppers, you can use all green ones; the taste is similar but just not as colorful.

Yield: 9 pints

Ingredients:

- 3 pounds yellow onions (4 cups ground)
- ½ large cabbage (4 cups ground)
- 10 large green tomatoes (4 cups ground)
- 5 pounds total green and red bell peppers (about 15 whole or 7 cups ground peppers)
- ½ cup pickling salt
- 6 cups white sugar
- 1 tablespoon celery seed
- 2 tablespoons mustard seed
- 1½ teaspoons turmeric
- 4 cups cider vinegar
- 2 cups water

1. Wash and grind each of the vegetables in a food grinder (using the coarse blade), or chop them very finely, to achieve the stated measurement. (Do not use a food processor.) Drain excess liquids.

2. Place the vegetables in a large pot, and mix them together. Sprinkle them with salt; cover the mixture loosely with a towel, and let it sit overnight.

3. Rinse the vegetables thoroughly—two times—to remove all salt, draining very well each time; place them in several layers of cheesecloth and squeeze out any excess water—the vegetables should be very dry; then set them aside.

4. Combine the remaining ingredients in a large pot, boil for 3 minutes, add the drained vegetables, return to a boil, and simmer for 3 minutes. Remove the pot from the heat.

5. Ladle the hot relish into jars, leaving a ¼-inch headspace. Add a small amount of liquid, if necessary, to get to a ¼-inch headspace.

6. Process the finished pints for 15 minutes.

Festive Corn Relish

Yield: 6 pints

Ingredients:

- 🍀 8 cups fresh whole-kernel corn (blanch about 18 ears for 5 minutes [see "All About Blanching in the appendix] and cut off the cob) or 8 cups frozen whole-kernel corn
- 🍀 1 small head cabbage, chopped (4 cups total)
- 🍀 1 medium onion chopped (1 cups total)
- 🍀 2 small green and 2 small red bell peppers, chopped (2 cups total)
- 🍀 4 cups white vinegar
- 🍀 1³/₄ cups sugar
- 🍀 1 cup water
- 🍀 2 tablespoons canning salt
- 🍀 2 tablespoons dry mustard
- 🍀 1 tablespoon celery seed
- 🍀 1 tablespoon whole mustard seed
- 🍀 1 tablespoon turmeric

1. Wash and cut, chop, or grind the vegetables to achieve the stated measurements for each.
2. Combine all ingredients in a large saucepan, bring to a boil, and simmer for 10 minutes.
3. Pack the hot relish into hot jars, leaving a ¹/₄-inch headspace. Add a small amount of syrup if necessary to reach the ¹/₄-inch headspace.
4. Process the finished pints for 15 minutes.

Beet Relish

Yield: 10 half-pints

Ingredients:

- 🍀 12 medium beets, cooked, peeled, and chopped (4 cups total)
- 🍀 2 small red bell peppers, chopped (1 cup total)
- 🍀 1 small head cabbage, chopped (4 cups total)
- 🍀 1 medium onion, chopped (1 cups total)
- 🍀 3 cups white vinegar
- 🍀 1¹/₂ cups sugar

- 1 tablespoon prepared horseradish
- 1 tablespoon canning salt

1. Wash, cook, peel (if necessary), and chop all vegetables to achieve the stated measurements for each.
2. Combine all ingredients in a large saucepan; bring it to a boil, stirring to mix; and simmer for 10 minutes.
3. Pack the hot vegetables into half-pint jars, leaving a ¼-inch headspace; add syrup if necessary to reach the ¼-inch headspace.
4. Process finished half-pints for 15 minutes.

SALSAS

Fiesta Salsa

Yield: 4 pints or 8 half-pints

Ingredients:

- 4 pounds fresh tomatoes (about 12 medium whole tomatoes or 9 cups diced) or 5 cans (14½-ounces) of diced tomatoes
- 1 packet Ball Fiesta Salsa Mix

1. Combine tomatoes and salsa mix in saucepan.
2. Heat to a boil; then reduce the heat and simmer for 5 minutes.
3. Pack hot salsa into hot jars, leaving a ½-inch headspace.
4. Process the finished jars: 35 minutes for both half-pints and pints.

Zesty Tomato/Pepper Salsa

When cutting and seeding hot peppers, remember to wear rubber gloves to prevent irritating your hands.

Yield: 6 pints

Ingredients:

- 6 pounds tomatoes, peeled, cored, seeded, and chopped (10 cups total)
- 2 pounds long green peppers (Italian frying), chopped and seeded (5 cups total)
- 1½ pounds yellow onions, peeled and chopped (5 cups total)
- 1 pound hot peppers, chopped and seeded (2½ cups total)
- 3 cloves garlic, minced
- 1¼ cups cider vinegar

- ❖ 3 tablespoons fresh cilantro, minced
- ❖ 1 tablespoon canning salt
- ❖ 1 teaspoon hot pepper sauce (optional)

1. Wash, peel, core, seed, and chop all vegetables to achieve the stated measurements for each.

2. Combine all ingredients in a large saucepan. Bring the mixture to a boil, stirring to combine the vegetables. Reduce the heat and simmer for 10 minutes.

3. Remove from heat and ladle hot salsa into hot jars, leaving a ¼-inch headspace; add hot liquid if necessary to the same ¼-inch headspace.

4. Process the finished pints for 15 minutes.

THE REFRIGERATOR-PICKLE PROCESS OVERVIEW

1. Thoroughly wash and sanitize your jars and lids, then keep them warm.

2. If necessary, prepare a spice bag.

3. Thoroughly wash all vegetables, cutting ¹⁄₁₆ inch off the blossom end. Cut, slice, chop, or grind the vegetables as directed in your recipe. Place them in a large glass, enamel, or stainless-steel bowl.

4. Combine vinegar or lemon with the other ingredients in a large stainless-steel or enamel pot, and bring this to a boil.

5. Pour pickling syrup over the vegetables.

6. Pack the vegetables into prepared jars, leaving a ½-inch headspace. Ladle syrup over the vegetables to the same ½-inch headspace. Apply the lids and refrigerate the jars.

7. Continue to store the jars in the refrigerator. Do no use them for at least twenty-four hours; for the best flavor, wait at least two weeks. Pickles will keep unopened for three months in the refrigerator.

Refrigerator Pickle Recipes

For each jar, allow the required headspace; wipe the rim clean; adjust the cap; and store the jar in the refrigerator.

Lois's No-Cook Refrigerator Sweet Pickles

Yield: 5 pints

Ingredients:

- 3 pounds pickling cucumbers
- 3½ cups sugar
- ¼ cup canning salt
- 2 cups white vinegar
- 3 medium onions, peeled and sliced (2 cups total)

1. Wash the cucumbers, cut off the blossom ends, and cut into ¼-inch slices. (Do not peel the cucumbers.) Set aside.

2. Combine the sugar, salt, and vinegar in a bowl, and let stand for 2 hours, stirring occasionally until the sugar is dissolved.

3. Place the cucumbers and onions in a bowl; pour the liquid over the vegetables.

4. Follow the directions in "The Refrigerator-Pickle Process Overview."

Refrigerated Dill Slices

Yield: 5 pints

Ingredients:

- 8 cups pickling cucumbers, trimmed and cut into ¼-inch slices
- 2 cups white vinegar
- 2 cups water
- 6 tablespoons pickling salt
- ¼ cup sugar
- 2 tablespoons pickling spice
- 7½ teaspoons dill seed
- 5 teaspoons whole mustard seed
- 1¼ teaspoons whole black peppercorn
- 6 cloves garlic, halved (optional)

1. Place the cucumber slices in a large bowl and set aside.

2. Combine the vinegar, water, salt, sugar, and pickling spice in a large saucepan. Bring this to a boil over medium-high heat, stirring to dissolve the sugar and salt. Reduce the heat and simmer for 10 minutes.

3. Pour the pickling liquid over the cucumbers. Cover the bowl with waxed paper or a clean cloth; set aside for 30 minutes or until it's cooled to room temperature.

4. In each jar, place $1\frac{1}{2}$ teaspoons of dill seed, 1 teaspoon of mustard seed, $\frac{1}{4}$ teaspoon of peppercorn, and 2 garlic-clove halves (optional). Add the cucumber slices, leaving a generous $\frac{1}{2}$-inch headspace. Ladle the pickling syrup over the cucumbers to the same $\frac{1}{2}$-inch headspace.

If you're bored with canned cranberry sauce, try your hand at cranberry chutney, the perfect twist on this traditional holiday accompaniment.

THE CHUTNEY AND SAUCE PROCESS

Chutneys and sauces are cooked for longer than other pickled products, and they develop thicker syrups as they simmer. Use a heavy-bottomed pot or Dutch oven to help prevent scorching, and stir often. Chutneys develop their flavor by standing for several weeks after being processed. For sauces, it may be necessary to add vinegar and some of the spices later in the cooking process.

1. Prepare your jars and water-bath canner, as well as a clean staging area.

2. Thoroughly wash all vegetables and fruits. Cut, slice, chop, or grind the vegetables as directed in your recipe, being careful not to chop them too finely.

3. If necessary, prepare a spice bag, adding it at the appropriate time.

4. Add the ingredients to a heavy stainless-steel or enamel pot or Dutch oven as directed in the recipe.

5. Simmer the ingredients slowly according to the directions until you achieve the desired consistency, reducing the temperature if necessary, to prevent scorching as the mixture thickens.

6. For sauces, puree the ingredients with a stick (immersion) blender or put them in a regular blender or food mill.

7. Also for sauces, adjust the ingredients and seasonings as indicated in the recipe.

8. When finished cooking, remove the chutney or sauce from the heat, pack it hot into hot jars, remove any bubbles, adjust the two-piece caps, and process the finished jars. See "Canning Pickled Products" on page 188.

Chutney and Sauce Recipes

For each jar, allow the required headspace; wipe the rim clean; adjust the cap; and process the jar for the amount of time stated.

CHUTNEYS

Curried Apple Chutney

This is great with Indian cuisine! Just remember: when cutting or chopping hot peppers, wear rubber gloves to prevent irritating your hands.

Yield: 10 pints

Ingredients:

* 16 medium firm, tart apples, peeled, cored, and chopped (8 cups total)
* 2 pounds raisins
* 4 cups light brown sugar
* 1 medium yellow onion, peeled and chopped (1 cup total)
* 2 small sweet red peppers, chopped (1 cup total)
* 3 tablespoons mustard seed
* 2 tablespoons ground ginger
* 2½ teaspoons ground allspice
* 2 teaspoons curry powder
* 2 teaspoons canning salt
* 2 hot red peppers, chopped
* 2 cloves garlic, minced
* 4 cups cider vinegar

1. Combine all ingredients in a large saucepan. Bring the mixture to a boil, reduce the heat, and simmer until thick, stirring frequently to prevent sticking.

2. Ladle the hot mixture into hot jars, leaving a ¼-inch headspace.

3. Process the finished pints in a water-bath canner for 10 minutes.

Plum Chutney

This chutney is both colorful and flavorful! Dress up the jar with a pretty ribbon for a great host/hostess gift.

Yield: 6 pints

Ingredients:

❖ 16 cups blue plums (Damson or Stanley), unpeeled, chopped, and pitted

❖ 3 cups light brown sugar, lightly packed

❖ 3 cups white vinegar

❖ 2½ cups raisins

❖ 1 medium yellow onion, peeled and chopped (1 cup total)

❖ 2 tablespoons whole mustard seed

❖ 2½ teaspoons ground ginger

❖ 1 teaspoon canning salt

1. Combine all ingredients in a large saucepan.

2. Bring the mixture to a boil, stirring frequently; reduce the heat and simmer, stirring often to prevent sticking, until mixture reaches desired consistency (about 30 minutes).

3. Ladle hot chutney into hot jars, leaving ½-inch headspace.

4. Process the finished pints for 10 minutes.

SAUCES

Ketchup

This ketchup is tangy and delicious and has no chemicals, no additives, and no high-fructose corn syrup. This is a great way to use your excess tomatoes and eat healthy. Expect to stick around the house when you make this because it does take some time to cook it to the right consistency.

Yield: 6 pints

Ingredients:

❋ 48 large tomatoes, cored and chopped (32 cups total)

❋ 2 medium yellow onions, peeled and chopped (2 cups total)

❋ 2 medium red bell pepper, chopped (1 cup total)

❋ 1 tablespoon celery seed

❋ 2½ teaspoons whole allspice

- 2 teaspoons whole mustard seed
- 2 sticks cinnamon
- 2 cups sugar
- 2 tablespoons canning salt
- 2 tablespoons paprika
- 3 cups cider vinegar

1. Wash, peel, core, and chop the vegetables to achieve the stated measurements of each.

2. Combine the tomatoes, onions, and peppers in a large saucepan. Bring them to a boil; then reduce the heat and simmer until the tomatoes are tender.

3. Strain the cooked vegetables through a food mill to puree them and remove the tomato skins and seeds. Return the puree to the saucepan and cook rapidly, stirring frequently, until the puree is thick and reduced by half.

4. Tie the whole spices in the spice bag. Add the spice bag, sugar, salt, and paprika to the puree. Simmer this for about 25 minutes, stirring frequently.

5. Add the vinegar, return the puree just to a boil, and then simmer it, stirring frequently, until you reach the desired consistency. Remove it from the heat. Remove (and compost) the spice bag.

6. Ladle the hot ketchup into hot jars, leaving a ¼-inch headspace.

7. Process the finished pints for 10 minutes.

Southwestern Barbecue Sauce

This one's indispensable when grilling! It's tangy, with shades of the Southwest thanks to a few jalapeño peppers. Remember, when cutting or chopping hot peppers, wear rubber gloves to prevent irritating your hands.

Yield: 5 pints

Ingredients:

- 30 tomatoes, cored and chopped (20 cups total)
- 2 cups celery, chopped and leafy ends removed
- 2 medium onions, peeled and chopped (2 cups total)

* 1½ cups green bell peppers, seeded and chopped
* 2 jalapeño peppers, seeded and chopped
* 1 teaspoon whole black peppercorns
* 2½ cups white vinegar
* 1½ cups light brown sugar, lightly packed
* 2 cloves garlic, finely chopped
* 4 teaspoons dry mustard
* 1 tablespoon paprika
* 2 teaspoons hot pepper sauce
* 1½ teaspoons canning salt

1. Combine the tomatoes, celery, onions, and green and jalapeño peppers in a large saucepan. Bring them to a boil over high heat, stirring frequently. Reduce the heat, cover the pan, and continue the boil until all vegetables are soft, about 30 minutes.

2. Working in batches, if necessary, strain the tomato-vegetable mixture through a food mill to puree it and remove the tomato skins and seeds.

3. Return the puree to the saucepan, return it to a boil, and then simmer it, stirring frequently, until the mixture is reduced by half (about 45 minutes).

4. Tie the peppercorns in a spice bag.

5. Add the vinegar, brown sugar, garlic, mustard, paprika, hot pepper sauce, salt, and spice bag to the tomato puree. Increase the heat to medium and boil the puree gently, stirring frequently, for about 1 hour or until the mixture is thickened to a consistency somewhat thinner than commercial barbeque sauce.

6. Remove and compost the spice bag.

7. Remove the sauce from the heat. Ladle it hot into hot jars, leaving a ½-inch headspace.

8. Process the finished pints for 35 minutes.

MAKING FERMENTED (LONG-BRINE) PICKLES AND SAUERKRAUT

Dill pickles and sauerkraut have very similar processes that involve fermenting in a salt (or salt-and-vinegar) brine. Lactic fermentation is a very old form of preservation and can be used for many types of vegetables, but we'll keep our focus on pickles and sauerkraut.

A reminder about the crock that you'll use for fermenting the pickles or sauerkraut: If you have a good earthen crock, that's great, but food-grade plastic or glass tubs also work well. Whichever you choose, make sure that it's deep enough to allow at least 4 to 5 inches between the vegetable and the rim of the crock.

Long-Brine Pickle Recipes

Can't you just taste the grilled Reuben sandwich with your sauerkraut inside and your deli dill sitting next to it, waiting to steal the show? You may have to wait a while for the pleasure, but it will be well worth it.

"Deli-Style" Dill Pickles

The quantities below will work with a 1-gallon crock and will yield about 5 pints or 2 quarts. (Generally, figure about 3 to 4 cucumbers per pint.) Multiply as desired for a larger crock and larger yields.

Yield: 5 pints or 2 quarts

Ingredients:

❧ 4 pounds of 4-inch cucumbers

❧ ½ cup pickling salt

❧ ¼ cup white vinegar (5% acidity)

❧ 8 cups water

❧ 2 whole cloves garlic (optional)

❧ 2 tablespoons dill seed or 5 heads of fresh or dry dill weed

❧ 2 teaspoons whole pickling spice (optional)

1. Clean the cucumbers, removing ¹⁄₁₆ inch from the blossom ends.

2. Make the brine by dissolving the salt in vinegar and water.

3. Peel the cloves and separate them into sections (optional).

4. Place half of the dill and optional spices at the bottom of the crock. Add the cucumbers and then the remaining dill and spices.

5. Cover the cucumbers completely with brine, using a weighted lid or plate to keep the cucumbers submerged under the brine. To make a good weight, fill two or three quart jars with water and cap them. Place the jars on top of the plate or lid. Cover the crock loosely with a cloth. Store it in a location that will maintain a consistent temperature—ideally, 70°F. If stored at a lower temperature, fermentation will be slower and take longer. Do not store the crock below 55 degrees.

6. Check your pickles every day, removing any scum that forms on the top. If you don't remove the scum, it can lower the acidity of the brine, and the pickles will spoil. *If the pickles become slimy, soft, or smelly, then stop everything and discard them. They have spoiled.*

7. You will know that the pickles are fermenting because you'll see bubbles rising to the top. When the bubbles have stopped forming, tap gently on the side of the crock. If no bubbles come to the surface, fermentation is complete. If bubbles come to the top, continue fermenting.

8. When it appears fermentation is complete, test a pickle by cutting it in half. It should have a consistent, dark-green color, with no white spots or rings that would indicate incomplete fermentation.

9. Pickles can be stored in a crock for 4 to 6 months or processed in a water-bath canner to keep for up to a year.

10. If leaving the pickles whole, prick them in a few spots to prevent shriveling.

11. If processing the pickles, remove them from the brine. Pour the brine into a stainless-steel or enamel pot, bring it to a boil, cook for 5 minutes, and then strain it through a coffee filter or several layers of cheesecloth to remove any sediment. Pack the pickles into hot jars, leaving a 1/2-inch headspace. Fill the jars with hot brine to the same 1/2-inch headspace, remove any bubbles, adjust the caps, and process the finished jars: 10 minutes for pints and 15 minutes for quarts.

Check your pickles every day to remove any scum that forms on the top.

MAKING SAUERKRAUT

We'll keep things very simple for sauerkraut because it's really just cabbage and salt. You'll find some fancier recipes out there that spice it up with herbs or red cabbage, but I suggest, for your first foray, to stay basic. That way, you'll have a good idea of what to expect at the end, in terms of flavor and color. As with fermented pickles, having very fresh cabbage is essential. Although cabbage will keep for weeks if you're planning to use it for coleslaw or cooked cabbage, you'll want cabbage that was sitting in the garden yesterday for sauerkraut.

While fermented pickles involve making a separate brine from salt, water, and sometimes vinegar, with sauerkraut, you gently mix the salt with the shredded cabbage to wilt it and draw out the juices, thus forming its own brine. You'll do this mixing just with your clean hands; if your hands are sensitive, you can wear rubber gloves. Let the cabbage rest for a few minutes while mixing, and you'll see that the salt will have drawn out more liquid from the cabbage. If your cabbage doesn't have enough natural juices to make a brine that covers the cabbage when you pack it into the crock, you may need to add some extra brine. Make this by boiling 1½ tablespoons of pickling or canning salt to each quart of water. (This will begin to make more sense when you read the recipe.) Cutting the cabbage is pretty important, too. Folks who do this a lot invest in a mandolin food slicer. This will help ensure evenly sized shreds of cabbage. But a good, sharp kitchen knife will work just fine. Make sure you cut out the heart of the cabbage and make thin slices (about 1/16-inch thick, or the thickness of a quarter).

Whether you like a little sauerkraut on your hot dog or just a scoop as a side dish, you'll enjoy it better when it's homemade.

Sauerkraut Recipe

Yield: 12 pints or 6 quarts

Ingredients:

❖ 25 pounds of cabbage

❖ $^3/_4$ cup canning or pickling salt,

❖ Additional brine, if needed

1. Work with about 5 pounds of cabbage at a time. Remove the outer leaves, then wash and rinse the cabbage thoroughly. Cut the heads into fourths and remove the hard cores.

2. Slice the cabbage thinly (with the grain) to produce long, $^1/_{16}$-inch thick threads (not short "Dixie" or "Cross-Cut" pieces).

3. Put 5 pounds of cabbage shreds and 3 tablespoons of canning salt into a large stainless-steel, plastic, or glass bowl. Work in the salt to draw out the juices, then pack the cabbage firmly into your crock. The brine must cover the cabbage.

4. Repeat in 5 pound batches until all the cabbage is salted and packed into the crock and is covered with brine. Add additional brine if necessary.

5. Add a lid and weights to keep the cabbage completely submerged below the brine. To make a good weight, fill two or three quart jars with water and cap them. Place the jars on top of the plate or lid. Cover the crock loosely with a cloth.

6. Store the crock in a location that will maintain a consistent temperature—ideally, 70 to 75°F. If stored at a lower temperature, fermentation will be slower and take longer. Do not store below 60°F. Depending upon the temperature, it will take between 3 and 6 weeks to ferment.

7. Check for fermentation activity every few days and remove any scum that forms on the top. If the brine level drops, add more brine to keep the kraut covered.

8. When the fermentation is complete, you can store sauerkraut in a covered container in the refrigerator for up to 3 months, or process it as follows using a water-bath canner:

   • **To hot-pack:** Bring the kraut and brine to a boil, stirring frequently. Remove it from the heat; pack the kraut and juice firmly into jars, leaving a $^1/_2$-inch headspace. Adjust the lids and process the finished jars: 10 minutes for pints and 15 minutes for quarts, adjusting for altitude (see the section "Altitude Adjustment" in the appendix).

   • **To raw-pack:** Pack the kraut and juice into jars, leaving a $^1/_2$-inch headspace. Adjust the lids and process the finished jars: 20 minutes for pints and 25 minutes for quarts, adjusting for altitude.

CANNING PICKLED PRODUCTS

For detailed instructions on water-bath canning, see chapter 4. Here are the highlights:

1. Prepare your jars, lids, and bands. Keep the jars and lids warm.

CANNING EQUIPMENT RECAP

Here's a quick list of what you need for water-bath canning. Check out chapter 4 for detailed information.

- ❖ Water-bath canner with rack
- ❖ Mason jars: Pint and quart size are preferred. Wide-mouth jars are helpful for large pickles.
- ❖ Lids and screw bands
- ❖ Canning funnel
- ❖ Jar lifter
- ❖ Lid lifter
- ❖ Bubble probe
- ❖ Clean cloths

2. Prepare your water-bath canner, bringing the water to a boil prior to placing the jars in the bath. (This is different from other canning instructions that call for placing jars in simmering water.)

3. Make the pickled product according to your recipe.

4. One jar at a time, fill the hot jar with the pickled product and syrup, leaving the required headspace. Wipe the rim clean using a clean, damp cloth; place the lid; and adjust the two-piece cap.

5. Place the finished jars in the water-bath canner as they are filled.

6. When the canner is full, make sure the jars are covered with 1 to 2 inches of water. Place the lid on the canner, bring the water to a boil, and continue to boil gently for the required amount of time, adjusting as necessary for altitude (see "Altitude Adjustment" in the appendix).

7. After the processing time is complete, turn off the heat, remove the lid from the canner, and wait 5 minutes.

8. Remove the jars from the canner, placing them on a rack or a layer of towels, away from any drafts. Do not tighten or touch the bands.

9. Label, date, and store pickled products for up to a year.

IF IT DOESN'T LOOK JUST LIKE THE PICTURE

When you are ready to use your pickles and such, you may find that they didn't turn out exactly as you had hoped. In most cases, it's a matter of them not being as crisp or tasty as you might like. In the list below, you'll find some of the problems you may encounter and their possible causes. Because many of these products are made using low-acid vegetables, be sure to check carefully for signs of spoilage. While this is rare, if any of the jars are seeping or bulging, do not open or taste them. See "Store and Enjoy" on page 110 in chapter 4 for details about handling spoiled food.

Here are some of the common problems in pickling and their likely causes. Fortunately, most conditions can be prevented.

❖ **Hollow pickles.** The cucumbers were hollow to begin with. When washing the cucumbers, you can identify those with hollow centers because they will float.

❖ **Dark or discolored pickles.** This can be caused by using hard water, reactive cooking utensils (brass, iron, copper, aluminum, or zinc), or using ground spices when whole spices were called for, as well as leaving dark spices such as cloves and cinnamon sticks in the jar while the food is processing.

❖ **Dull or faded pickles.** This can be caused by using poor-quality cucumbers, insufficient brining, or excessive exposure to light during storage.

❖ **Shriveled pickles.** A number of possible causes exist here, including not pricking whole pickles; adding too much salt, sugar, or vinegar to the cucumbers at one time; using waxed cucumbers; overcooking; or overprocessing.

❖ **Soft or slippery pickles.** This applies to fermented pickles. If there is any sign of spoilage or foul odor, discard them. There are many reasons for soft or slippery pickles, including not removing the blossom end, the brine being too weak, not removing the scum from the brine daily, not covering the pickles completely with brine, and underprocessing pickles.

❖ **Cloudy pickle juice.** Underprocessing, using hard water, or using table salt with anti-caking ingredients can all cause this.

❖ **Pickles not crisp.** This can be caused by using the wrong type of cucumber, using a poor-quality one, or using a cucumber that is not fresh (older than twenty-four hours).

❖ **White sediment in the bottom of the jars.** A small amount of sediment is harmless and can be caused by yeasts that have settled at the bottom or by using table salt with additives.

Cut your cucumbers lengthwise in quarter-inch slices for perfect sandwich-type pickles.

LABELING AND STORAGE

Congratulations! You are now a pickle or relish maker, and you have a new talent for your home-preservation repertoire. As with other canned goods, check to make sure that the jars are sealed, remove the band, wipe the jar to remove any food particles, and label jars with their contents, date, and batch. If jars haven't sealed after twenty-four hours, store them in the refrigerator and use their contents soon. Add finished and sealed jars to your canning inventory, and then store them in a cool, dry place for up to a year—that's if you can resist the urge to enjoy some right now! When you are ready to use the jarred food, be sure to check carefully for signs of spoilage. Again, see "Store and Enjoy" in chapter 4 for details about the canning inventory and optimal storage conditions.

TECHNIQUES

You'll want to dog-ear this page so that you can come back to it while you're trying out the recipes in chapters 3 through 6. You'll see references to such techniques as blanching, treating for discoloration, and preparing sugar syrups several times throughout those chapters, and until these techniques become second-nature, you'll want to reference this section. I've also included pressure-canning processing times for popular fruits and vegetables, a chart illustrating the adjustments you'll need to make if you live above sea level, and a sample food inventory.

ALL ABOUT BLANCHING

Blanching is submerging a fruit or vegetable in rapidly boiling water or steam for a specific length of time. This accomplishes several important tasks for vegetables (and some fruits) and is required for all vegetables that you plan to freeze for longer than four weeks because it stops the enzyme action, which, if left unchecked, changes the texture and quality of the vegetable. This is not so for fruits. Generally, the only reason to blanch fruit is to help loosen the skin, such as with peaches. Blanching also helps to clean off surface dirt that you might have missed when washing. It also removes bacteria, yeasts, and molds. Finally, blanching brightens the color of the vegetable.

Different fruits and vegetables require different lengths of time for blanching. The timing is important: too short and you haven't stopped those pesky enzymes; too long and you lose nutrients and create a soft product. Always follow your recipes' instructions for proper timing.

There are three different ways to blanch. Each of these requires that you thoroughly clean and prepare the produce.

❖ **Boiling-water blanching.** Bring at least 1 gallon of water to a rapid boil in a large pot. A good ratio to use is 1 gallon of water to 1 pound of produce. Using a blanching basket, submerge about 1 pound of produce at a time into the water. Once the water returns to a boil, begin timing according to the recipe. Remove the produce from the boiling water and submerge it immediately into ice water to stop the cooking. Drain well.

❖ **Steam blanching.** Put 1 inch of water into a large steaming pot (one with a basket) and bring the water to a rolling boil. Place one pound of produce in the basket and place it in the pot; cover the pot with a lid. Time the steaming according to the chart. Remove the basket and

submerge it immediately into ice water to stop the cooking. Drain well.

❖ **Microwave blanching.** Pour ¼ cup of water into a round, microwave-safe bowl. Place no more than 2 cups of veggies (4 cups if you're blanching only the leafy type) into the bowl. Cover the bowl with microwave-safe plastic wrap, allowing at least 1 inch of space between the food and the plastic. Microwave on the highest setting for the time specified in the recipe. Remove the bowl from the microwave, and remove the plastic wrap from the side of the bowl that is facing away from you to vent any hot steam. Submerge the vegetables in ice water to stop the cooking. Drain well.

Of the three media, boiling water and steam are much preferred because the power levels of microwaves differ considerably.

If you don't have a blanching basket, you can put the veggies directly into the boiling water. When the boiling time is finished, either remove the produce using a slotted spoon or drain off the boiling water, being very careful to pour away from you to avoid the hot steam. Of course, draining off the water will only work for blanching one batch of veggies. If blanching more than one batch of the same vegetables, you will want to keep the water rather than heating a new batch.

TREATING FOR DISCOLORATION

Some light-colored fruits such as apples, peaches, pears, apricots, and nectarines darken and become unappetizing when exposed to air, both before and during freezing. There are a number of products available to pre-treat fruits to prevent discoloration. The two most popular are a commercially available crystalline ascorbic acid mixture (the most common is Fruit-Fresh Produce Protector) or plain ascorbic acid, either in crystalline form or as vitamin C tablets that have been crushed. Other, less-satisfactory methods are crystalline citric acid and lemon juice.

I highly recommend using Fruit-Fresh or a similar commercially prepared product. The ease of use and measurement make it well worth any slight additional cost. If your local grocery doesn't stock Fruit-Fresh, you can find many online suppliers (see Resources). If you prefer to use ascorbic acid tablets (vitamin C that you can find at your local pharmacy), crush the tablets to form a powder. You will need 3,000 milligrams of vitamin C to create 1 teaspoon of ascorbic acid.

If using citric acid, you will need three times as much as ascorbic acid. If using lemon juice, you will need six times as much as ascorbic acid. For both citric acid and lemon juice, you run the risk of tainting the flavor of the fruit. This is not a problem with ascorbic acid.

Here are the common methods for using the ascorbic acid:

❖ Mix the required amount with a few tablespoons of water and apply directly to the fruit.

❖ Mix the required amount with the sugar and then mix the combination with the fruit.

❖ Add the required amount to the syrup when preparing it.

PREPARING SUGAR SYRUPS

When preparing syrup packs for either canning or freezing, use the proportions below. You may use honey for part of the syrup, though it will influence the flavor of the fruit. To prepare the syrup, combine the ingredients in a pan and bring them to a boil. Simmer the mixture until the sugar is completely dissolved. Depending upon the syrup's intended use, either cool it or use it while hot. You will need approximately ½ to ¾ cups of syrup for each pint and 1 to 1½ cups for each quart that you can.

TYPE OF SYRUP	PERCENTAGE OF SUGAR	CUPS OF SUGAR	CUPS OF HONEY	CUPS OF WATER	YIELD IN CUPS OF SYRUP
Extra-light	20	1½	0	5½	6
Light	30	2¼	0	5¼	6½
Medium	40	3¼	0	5	7
Heavy	50	4¼	0	4¼	7
Honey	0	1	1	4	5

THE ART OF THE JELLY BAG

The secret to beautiful and flavorful jelly is separating the juice from the skin and pulp. You'll need a lot more fruit to make jelly than you do to make jam. To get about 1 cup of juice, you'll need about 3½ cups of berries or soft fruit or about one pound of hard fruit, such as apples or peaches. Here's how to extract the juice:

1. Wash and drain the fruit. For hard fruit like apples, cut it into quarters and remove the stem and blossom ends. Do not peel or remove cores. It's okay to remove pits. For berries and grapes, drain and handle them gently to avoid breaking them and losing any of the precious juice!

2. Put the fruit in a large stainless-steel pot with about ¼ cup of water for each quart of berries or 1 cup of water for each pound of hard fruit. Use just enough water to prevent scorching; use too much and you'll have watery jelly.

3. Bring the pot to a gentle boil, stirring to crush the fruit. Cook berries and grapes about 10 minutes or until just tender. Cook apples and other hard fruits 20–25 minutes.

4. While the fruit is cooking, set up your jelly bag (or colander lined with cheesecloth) so that it will be suspended over a deep bowl that catches the juice as it drains. Dampen the jelly bag slightly so that it doesn't absorb too much of the fruit juice.

5. Transfer the fruit to the jelly bag, handling it carefully, as the mixture will be very hot. Suspend the jelly bag over the bowl and let it drip for at least 2 hours or as long as overnight. Resist the urge to squeeze the bag to extract more juice. It will be very tempting, but we're looking

for quality here, not quantity. If you force out the juice, you'll get some of the pulp—your jelly will be cloudy and you won't win first prize at the county fair. If that doesn't matter to you, the cloudiness does not have any adverse effects.

PRESSURE-CANNING PROCESSING TIMES

As mentioned in chapter 4, high-acid foods can be and usually are processed using the water-bath method. Some of these foods are quite suitable for pressure canning, as well. Pressure canning has some advantages in that it generally takes less time and less energy (you're heating less water), and some people feel that the foods keep their flavor and texture better. Follow the recipe and instructions for water-bath canning these foods, but substitute the pressure-canning processing times and pressures given below. Adjust as necessary for altitude.

TYPE OF FRUIT	HOT- OR RAW-PACK	PROCESSING TIME FOR PINTS (IN MINUTES)	PROCESSING TIME FOR QUARTS (IN MINUTES)	CANNER PRESSURE (DIAL GAUGE, IN PSI)	CANNER PRESSURE (WEIGHTED GAUGE, IN PSI)
Applesauce	Hot	8	10	6	5
Apples, sliced	Hot	8	8	6	5
Berries, whole	Hot	8	8	6	5
Berries, whole	Raw	8	10	6	5
Cherries	Hot	8	10	6	5
Cherries	Raw	10	10	6	5
Fruit purees	Hot	8	8	6	5
Peaches, apricots, and nectarines	Hot or raw	10	10	6	5
Pears	Hot	10	10	6	5
Plums	Hot or raw	10	10	6	5
Rhubarb	Hot	8	8	6	5
Tomato juice	Hot	20	20	6	5
Tomatoes crushed, no added liquid	Hot	20	20	6	5
Tomatoes, whole or halved, packed in water	Hot or raw	15	15	6	5
Tomatoes, whole or halved, packed without added water	Raw	40	40	6	5

ALTITUDE ADJUSTMENT

Just as in other types of cooking, if you live in higher altitudes, you will need to adjust the recipes for canning accordingly to ensure safe processing. The processing times given in the recipes are for locations at or below 1,000 feet above sea level. If you live more than 1,000 feet above sea level, use one of the charts below, depending upon whether you are water-bath or pressure canning.

ALTITUDE ADJUSTMENT FOR WATER-BATH CANNING

ALTITUDE (IN FEET)	MINUTES TO ADD TO NORMAL PROCESSING
0–1,000	0
1,001–3,000	5
3,001–6,000	10
6,001–8,000	15
8,001–10,000	20

ALTITUDE ADJUSTMENT FOR PRESSURE CANNING

ALTITUDE (IN FEET)	PRESSURE (IN PSI) FOR PROCESSING IN WEIGHTED-GAUGE CANNER	PRESSURE (IN PSI) FOR PROCESSING IN DIAL-GAUGE CANNER
0–1,000	10	11
1,001–2,000	15	11
2,001–4,000	15	12
4,001–6,000	15	13
6,001–8,000	15	14
8,001–10,000	15	15

SAMPLE INVENTORY

Here's a snippet from my canning inventory. I separate the fruits, vegetables, soft spreads, and pickled products, but you can organize it any way that works for you. I do mine on a spreadsheet on my computer, but paper and pencil works just fine, too. The columns are pretty self-explanatory, except for "Batch." Only use this if you make more than one batch of a particular food. The comments column is handy if there's something about that food that you want to remember or take note of.

Sample Inventory

FRUITS	Date	Batch	Exp. Date	Quart	Pint	Half-Pint	4-ounce	Comments
Applesauce	20111012	1	20121012	5	7			Used only McIntosh—no sugar. Good for kids
Applesauce	20111020	2	20121020		7			Used combination of Winesap and Fuji
Blueberries	20110801		20120801		3			Picked from Rose's
Blueberry syrup	20110801	1	20120801		2			From garden
Blueberry syrup	20110815	2	20120815	1				From garden
Peaches	20110825		20120825	8				

SOFT SPREADS	Date	Batch	Exp. Date	Quart	Pint	Half-Pint	4-ounce	Comments
Raspberry jam	20110705	1	20120705			7		Used Suzy's recipe
Raspberry jam	20110712	2	20120712			7		Used new recipe from Dottie
Raspberry jam	20110720	3	20120720				12	Used own recipe
Raspberry jam, seedless	20110725	1	20120725				7	
Strawberry jam	20110706	1	20120606		7			
Grape jelly	20110820	1	20120820			7		

VEGETABLES	Date	Batch	Exp. Date	Quart	Pint	Half-Pint	4-ounce	Comments
Beans (green)	20110712	1	20120712		7			
Beans (wax)	20110730		20120730					
Corn	20110915		20120915		20			

CONVERSIONS, QUANTITIES, AND EQUIVALENTS

How much is enough? How big is a bushel? How many ears does it take to can a quart? How many teaspoons to a tablespoon? This section is where you will find answers to those questions and more. For the charts discussing the yields of popular fruits and vegetables, quantities and equivalents are approximate and may vary with the size of the fruit or vegetable.

Fahrenheit to Celsius Conversion

Here are some of the common Celsius equivalents for the Fahrenheit temperatures given throughout the book:

DESCRIPTION	DEGREES FAHRENHEIT	DEGREES CELSIUS
Temperature for pressure canning	240	116
Water boils	212	100
Average simmer; bacteria, yeasts, and molds are killed, but some spores survive	190	88
Heat-resistant bacteria thrive	145	63
Temperature for drying foods	140	60
A nice, hot bath	104	40
Normal body temperature	98.6	37
Off to the beach!	86	30
Active growth for molds, yeasts, and bacteria	80	27
Room temperature	70	21
Cool day	50	10
Water freezes	32	0
Safe temperature for freezing food, or a very cold day	0	-18
Temperature to flash-freeze food	-10	-23

Fruit Yields (Canning & Freezing)

FRUIT	AMOUNT OF RAW FRUIT	YIELD (IN QUARTS)	-OR- POUNDS NEEDED PER QUART
Apples	1 bushel (48 pounds)	16	3
Apples (for sauce)	1 bushel (48 pounds)	14	$3\frac{1}{2}$
Apricots	1 lug (24 pounds)	12	2
Berries (except strawberries and cranberries)	24-quart flat (36 pounds)	12	2
Cherries	1 lug (15 pounds)	7	2
Grapes	1 lug (23 pounds)	10	2
Nectarines	1 flat (18 pounds)	7	$2\frac{1}{2}$
Peaches	1 bushel (50 pounds)	20	$2\frac{1}{2}$
Pears	1 bushel (50 pounds)	20	$2\frac{1}{2}$
Plums	1 bushel (56 pounds)	22	$2\frac{1}{2}$
Strawberries	24-quart crate (36 pounds)	12	$2\frac{1}{2}$
Tomatoes	2 flats/1 bushel (53 pounds)	20	$2\frac{1}{2}$
Tomatoes (for juice)	2 flats/1 bushel (53 pounds)	17	3

Fluid Measure Conversions

	TEA-SPOON	TABLE-SPOON	FLUID OUNCE	GILL	CUP	PINT	QUART	GALLON
Teaspoon	1	$\frac{1}{3}$	$\frac{1}{6}$	$\frac{1}{24}$	$\frac{1}{48}$	—	—	—
Tablespoon	3	1	$\frac{1}{2}$	$\frac{1}{8}$	$\frac{1}{16}$	$\frac{1}{32}$	—	—
Fluid Ounce	6	2	1	$\frac{1}{4}$	$\frac{1}{8}$	$\frac{1}{16}$	$\frac{1}{32}$	—
Gill	4	8	4	1	$\frac{1}{2}$	$\frac{1}{4}$	$\frac{1}{8}$	$\frac{1}{32}$
Cup	48	16	8	2	1	$\frac{1}{2}$	$\frac{1}{4}$	$\frac{1}{16}$
Pint	96	32	16	4	2	1	$\frac{1}{2}$	$\frac{1}{8}$
Quart	192	64	32	8	4	2	1	$\frac{1}{4}$
Gallon	768	256	128	32	16	8	4	1
Firkin	6912	2304	1152	288	144	72	36	9
Hogshead	48384	16128	8064	2016	1008	504	252	63

Vegetable Yields (Canning and Freezing)

VEGETABLE	AMOUNT OF RAW VEGETABLE	YIELD (IN QUARTS)	-OR- POUNDS NEEDED PER QUART
Asparagus	1 bushel (24 pounds)	9	$2\frac{1}{2}$
Beans, Lima (in pod)	1 bushel (30 lbs)	7	4
Beans, Green	1 bushel (39 pounds)	15	$1\frac{1}{2}$
Beets (without tops)	1 sack (25 pounds)	10	$2\frac{1}{2}$
Broccoli	1 crate (25 pounds)	10	$2\frac{1}{2}$
Cabbage	1 sack (50 lbs)	18	$2\frac{1}{2}$
Carrots	1 bushel (50 pounds)	18	$2\frac{1}{2}$–3
Cauliflower	11/2 bushel crate (37 pounds)	16	2 medium heads
Corn (in husks)	1 bushel (35 pounds)	8 (cut off cob)	3–6
Cucumbers	1 bushel (48 pounds)	26	$1\frac{1}{2}$–2
Eggplant	1 bushel (33 pounds)	16	2
Greens (chard, kale, collard, spinach, and so on)	1 bushel (18 pounds)	8	2–3
Peas (in pod, to be shelled)	1 bushel (30 pounds)	7	4–5
Peppers	1 bushel (25 pounds)	19	$1\frac{1}{3}$
Potatoes	1 bushel (60 pounds)	20	$2\frac{1}{2}$–3
Squash (summer)	1 box (40 pounds)	24	2

Miscellaneous Measurements

MEASURE	EQUIVALENT
1 dash	$\frac{1}{4}$ teaspoon or less
1 pinch	$\frac{1}{8}$ teaspoon or less
Juice of 1 lemon	2 to 3 tablespoons
Juice of 1 orange	About $\frac{1}{2}$ cup

Measure Conversions

IF YOU HAVE...	YOU ALSO HAVE...
1 tablespoon	3 teaspoons
1/16 cup	1 tablespoon
1/8 cup	2 tablespoons
1/6 cup	2 tablespoons + 2 teaspoons
1/4 cup	4 tablespoons
1/3 cup	5 tablespoons + 1 teaspoon
3/8 cup	6 tablespoons
1/2 cup	8 tablespoons
2/3 cup	10 tablespoons + 2 teaspoons
3/4 cup	12 tablespoons
1 cup	48 teaspoons
1 cup	16 tablespoons
8 fluid ounces	1 cup
1 pint	2 cups
1 quart	2 pints
4 cups	1 quart
1 gallon	4 quarts
16 ounces	1 pound
1 milliliter	1 cubic centimeter

Equivalents of Commonly Used Ingredients

INGREDIENT	ORIGINAL FORM	EQUIVALENT MEASUREMENTS
Ascorbic acid (Vitamin C):	3,000mg tablet	1 teaspoon powdered
Dill	1 head fresh dill	2 teaspoon dill seed
Garlic	1 small clove	1/2 teaspoon minced
	1 medium clove	1 teaspoon minced
Lemon	1 medium	2–3 tablespoons juice
	1 medium	2 tablespoons grated rind (lemon zest)
	5–6 medium	1 cup juice
Orange	1 medium	5–6 tablespoons juice
	1 medium	2 tablespoons grated rind (orange zest)
	3–4 medium	1 cup juice
Sugar	5 pounds, granulated	about 11 1/4 cups
	1 pound, granulated	about 2 1/4 cups
	1 pound, packed brown	about 2 1/4 cups

GLOSSARY

alum: Potassium aluminum sulfate, an ingredient used in older pickling recipes to add crispness and firmness to pickles. If using, follow directions carefully because it may cause nausea or gastrointestinal problems if consumed in large quantities.

acid foods: Foods that contain enough acid to result in a pH of 4.6 or lower. Includes all fruits except figs; most tomatoes; fermented and pickled vegetables; relishes; and jams, jellies, and marmalades. Acidic foods may be processed in a boiling water bath.

altitude adjustment: Adjusting the cooking or processing time to reflect the effect on boiling point caused by elevation above sea level. Water boils at a lower temperature the higher the elevation, thus processing times need to be increased.

antioxidant: In food preservation, an agent that prevents or controls oxidation, which causes the darkening or discoloration of light-colored fruits and vegetables.

ascorbic acid: Ascorbic acid is a naturally occurring sugar acid with antioxidant properties. It is usually white to yellowish white and is commonly known as vitamin C. Ascorbic acid is used in food preservation to retard discoloration in light-colored fruits and vegetables.

bacteria: Single-celled microorganisms, some helpful and some harmful, that are ubiquitous in nature. Harmful ones, such as *Salmonella*, *Clostridium botulinum*, and *E. coli* can cause spoilage and possibly food-borne illnesses in preserved foods. Heating to 240 degrees Fahrenheit destroys these bacteria and their spores.

band: *See* metal band.

blancher: A cooking pot fitted with a lid and a mesh or perforated basket. Food that is placed in the basket can be easily submerged and removed from boiling water or steam. Blanchers are used for loosening skins on fruits and tomatoes, or for heating foods to be hot-packed.

blanching: Dipping in boiling water or steam to slow the enzyme action in a vegetable or to loosen the skin of a fruit/vegetable prior to preservation.

boil: Raising the temperature of liquids, especially water, to 212 degrees Fahrenheit. When used in the context of home food preservation, "boil" means a full, rolling boil.

boiling water-bath canner: *See* water-bath canner.

botulism: The serious, sometimes deadly, food-borne illness caused by the toxins produced by the spores of the bacteria *Clostridium botulinum*. These spores, which are present in soil or dust clinging to raw produce, grow in low acid, anaerobic environments, such as that found in canned jars of low-acid foods. Pressure canning low-acid food at the specified temperature and pressure will destroy these spores and safely preserve the food.

BPA (Bisphenol A): This is an organic compound that is a building block of several important plastics and plastic additives, which are or have been used in numerous consumer products, including food and water containers. It is suspected of being harmful to humans, especially infants and children. Many food and beverage producers have voluntarily removed BPA from their containers.

brine: A solution of salt and water used in fermenting or pickling. Brines are made in different strengths, stated as the percentage of salt in the water.

bubble remover or probe: In canning, a thin nonmetallic instrument used to remove hidden bubbles from packed jars just prior to processing.

canner: A type of cooking vessel designed to boil or steam canned food for food preservation purposes. *See* water-bath canner *or* pressure canner.

canning: A method of home food preservation in which food is placed in sanitized jars, sealed with two-piece lids, processed to kill bacteria and seal the jar, and then stored at room temperature. There are two types of canning, boiling water bath and pressure. Also called "fresh preserving."

canning salt: Salt that has been specially prepared without iodine, anticaking, or other additives. These additives found in table salt can cause cloudy liquids or dark produce in canned foods. Also called "pickling salt."

citric acid: A organic acid that is a natural preservative, helps to raise the acidity level, and imparts a sour taste. Citric acid is often used in combination with ascorbic acid to prevent oxidation (discoloring) in light-colored fruits and vegetables.

cold-pack: *See* raw-pack.

cool place: When referring to storage of home-preserved foods, a "cool place" is expected to be between 50 and 70 degrees Fahrenheit.

dial-gauge pressure canner: One of two types of pressure canners, it is fitted with a one-piece pressure regulator and a gauge that visually indicates the pressure level inside the canner.

dry-pack: To pack without added liquid or sugar when freezing.

enzyme: A protein that causes chemical changes in organisms. In fruits and vegetables, enzymes cause changes in color, flavor, and texture. Canning stops the enzyme action; freezing and drying only slows it, thus vegetables to be frozen or dried must be blanched to stop the enzyme action.

exhausting: Using heat to force air from the jar while canning. Also refers to forcing air and steam from the pressure canner before sealing the vent or petcock.

fermentation: A process whereby bacteria, yeasts, or mold cause the conversion of sugars to acid or alcohol. Some types of fermentation are intentional and desired, such as lactic acid fermentation found in sauerkraut and fermented pickles. Some types of fermentation are undesirable and result in spoiled food. Bubbles are the most obvious sign of fermentation. If a canned product shows signs of unplanned fermentation, do not eat it.

fermented pickles: Cucumbers and other vegetables that are preserved using a long-brine method involving fermentation. The opposite of fermented pickles is fresh-pack pickles.

fingertip tight: A term that describes how tightly to twist when closing a two-piece cap on a canning jar. Screw closed until the cap is snug, but do not use a utensil or the full force of your hand.

flash freezing: Quickly freezing foods at temperatures of at least -10 degrees Fahrenheit to ensure safe and quality freezing. Some freezers have a flash-freeze or quick-freeze shelf for this purpose. Controlling how much you freeze at one time helps ensure this sub-zero temperature. Do not add at one time more than two to three pounds per cubic foot of freezer space.

food poisoning: A food-borne illness caused by the consumption of harmful bacteria and their toxins; symptoms are usually gastrointestinal and range from mild to (rarely) deadly.

freezer burn: Dehydration of the exterior of frozen foods resulting in loss of color, flavor, and texture. Freezer burn most often occurs when foods are improperly packed, leaving too much air inside the container.

fresh-pack pickled products: These are cucumbers and other pickled vegetables that are preserved in a spicy vinegar solution without fermenting, although they are frequently brined for several hours or overnight. All fresh-pack pickled products should stand for 4 to 6 weeks after processing to cure and develop optimal flavor. The opposite of fresh-pack is fermented.

fresh preserving: *See* canning.

gasket: A flexible rubber ring that sits inside the outer perimeter of a pressure canner lid, and provides a seal between the lid and the base so that steam cannot escape, thus building the necessary steam pressure.

gel or gel stage: The term used to describe the binding of water, sugar, acid, and pectin to form a jam-like consistency. The gelling point is 220 degrees Fahrenheit, or 8 degrees above the boiling point of water. Also called "set."

headspace: When filling a container with food to be processed or frozen, headspace is the distance between the top of the food and the top or rim of the container.

high-acid food: Foods that naturally have an acid level (pH) of 4.6 or lower. This includes most fruits and most tomatoes. The term "high-acid" also applies to foods whose acid level has been lowered by fermenting or adding acid. High-acid foods can safely be processed in a water-bath canner.

hot-pack: A canning procedure involving the heating of raw food in boiling water or steam before packing it hot into jars. Opposite of "raw-" or "cold-pack."

jar: A glass canning jar, often called a Mason jar, that has been designed with features needed for home canning, such as the ability to withstand repeated uses, as well as the high temperatures of pressure and water bath canning. They come in a variety of sizes and are sealed with specially designed two-piece caps consisting of lids and bands.

jar lifter: An hinged instrument used in canning that enables you to safely and securely lift hot jars in and out of hot canners. Gripping the hinged handle causes the lifter to hold the jar tighter.

lactic acid: The acid produced during fermentation. Salt interacts with the natural sugars in food to produce lactic acid, which then controls the growth of undesirable microorganisms by increasing the acidity of the food product. Lactic acid also adds a distinctive tart flavor to fermented foods, such as long-brine pickles.

lemon juice: The juice of a freshly squeezed lemon, or commercially prepared, bottled juice of lemons, often added to home-preserved foods, especially jams and jellies, to increase the acid levels. The acidity of freshly squeezed lemons is variable; bottled lemon juice is not. If a recipe specifies bottled lemon juice, do not substitute freshly squeezed.

lid: One part of the two-part sealing mechanism for modern canning, lids are round metal disks with a small band of sealing compound on the underside. They are held onto the top of the jar during canning by a circular, threaded metal ring or band. Lids are used only once.

long-brine fermentation: Soaking vegetables (usually cucumbers) in a brine made of salt, water, and sometimes vinegar for a long enough period of time (usually three to six weeks) for lactic fermentation to create sufficient lactic acid to preserve the low-acid vegetable safely.

low-acid foods: Foods that have little or no natural acid and have a pH above 4.6. The acidity in these foods is insufficient to prevent the growth of the bacterium *Clostridium botulinum, which can cause the food poisoning called botulism*. All vegetables, some tomatoes, figs, all meats, fish, seafoods, and dairy foods are low–acid foods.

low-methoxyl pectin: Pectin made from citrus peels that does not require sugar to produce a gel.

Mason jar: *See* jar.

metal band: A circular, threaded screw band used together with a flat metal lid to form a two-piece metal cap used for canning.

microorganisms: Organisms of microscopic size, including bacteria, yeasts, and molds. Some play a positive role, such as fermenting foods or creating antibiotics, while others can cause disease and food spoilage.

mold: Microscopic fungi that appear as fuzz on food. Molds thrive in an acidic environment and can produce dangerous mycotoxins, or reduce the acid level of the food.

mycotoxins: Toxins (poisons) produced by mold.

overnight: Eight to twelve hours.

paraffin wax: A pure, refined wax used in an outdated method for preserving soft spreads in which melted paraffin was poured over soft spreads and was believed to provide adequate prevention from contamination by microorganisms. The use of paraffin wax is not a safe or approved method for sealing soft spreads.

pasteurization: Heating a food to a temperature high enough to kill associated heat-resistant, disease-causing microorganisms. In food dehydrating, this involves heating meats to an internal temperature of 160 degrees Fahrenheit.

pectin: Pectin is a naturally occurring, complex set of polysaccharides found in the nonwoody portions of many plants, especially fruits, which is responsible for cell structure. When combined with sugar and acid, pectin helps to bind the water in fruit soft spreads forming a gel. Pectin is also available commercially in liquid or powdered forms and is used to make jams and jellies. See also low-methoxyl pectin.

petcock: The part of a dial gauge pressure canner that traps or releases the steam pressure.

pH: A measure of acidity or alkalinity with a scale ranging from 0 to 14 (acid to alkaline). A food is neutral when its pH is 7.0. Any foods with a pH of 4.6 or higher are low acid.

pickling: The process of preserving food, often cucumbers, in a high-acid solution that is created either through lactic fermentation or through the addition of salt and vinegar. Often, spices are added.

pickling salt: *See* canning salt.

pressure canner: A heavy-gauge cooking vessel designed to achieve high internal steam pressure and thus raise the temperature to 240 degrees Fahrenheit, a temperature high enough to kill bacteria and bacterial spores in low-acid foods. Pressure canners are the only safe way to can low-acid foods. Also called "steam pressure canner." The two common types are "dial gauge" and "weighted gauge."

pretreatment: A treatment prior to preserving that helps to slow enzyme action, and/or retard discoloration, and/or remove surface dirt and bacteria. Includes blanching and antioxidative treatments.

processing: A term generally applied to the steps involved in boiling water-bath and pressure canning. Processing destroys harmful microorganisms and aids in creating an air-tight seal.

processing time: In water-bath and pressure canning, the time for which filled jars must be heated in the boiling water or the pressurized steam. The processing time must be sufficient to heat the coldest spot in the jar to the required temperature. Recipes specify the processing time based on the size of the jar and the type and acidity of the food being preserved.

raw-pack: A canning procedure in which jars are filled with raw food. Also called "cold-pack." The opposite of raw-pack is "hot-pack."

reprocessing: Repeating the heat processing of a canned food product that did not seal within twenty-four hours. Reprocessing involves removing and discarding the original lid, reheating the food and/or liquid according to the recipe, repacking the food into clean jars with new lids and bands, and processing using the original method and time recommended by the recipe.

screw band: *See* metal band.

sealing compound: The tacky, shiny material found on the outside edge of the underside of jar lids. The sealing compound comes in contact with the rim of the jar, and forms a partial vacuum seal once the jar is cooled.

set: *See* gel.

short-brine: Soaking vegetables, usually cucumbers, is a brine solution of water, salt, and sometimes vinegar for a short time—from several hours to several days. This is long enough to begin to draw some of the sugar and moisture from the vegetable, but not long enough to start fermentation.

simmer: Cooking food gently at temperatures ranging from 180 to 200 degrees Fahrenheit.

skimmer (spoon): A flat, long-handled, slotted spoon used to skim foam from soft spreads after cooking or to drain liquid from cooked produce.

spice bag: A small cotton bag used to hold herbs and whole spices during cooking. When a spice bag is placed into cooking foods, only the flavor of the herbs and spices seep into the food or liquid, keeping the herbs and spices separate and easy to remove when cooking is finished. You can make an improvised spice bag by tying herbs and spices in several layers of cheesecloth.

spoilage: The growth of undesirable bacteria, molds, yeast, or other pathogens that can cause food-borne illness or reduce the quality of the food.

steam pressure canner: *See* pressure canning.

sterilization: The process of killing all living microorganisms.

syneresis: The separation of liquid from a gel. This can happen to jams and jellies during storage and is caused by the quantity of acid, the quality of the pectin, or improper storage conditions. While it may make the soft spread less appetizing, it poses no safety hazard.

syrup-pack: When freezing fruits, packing with a mixture of water or juice and sugar or other sweetener.

two-piece cap: A vacuum closure for home canning consisting of a metal lid with sealing compound and a circular, threaded band. Two-piece caps are sized to fit onto the top of canning jars.

vacuum packaging: A method of packaging food involving removal of air from the bag or container, and sealing the bag or container to prevent air from reentering. Heat may be used to seal the food, but not to process it. Vacuum-packaged foods must be refrigerated or frozen.

vacuum seal: The air-tight seal that is created when canning foods. Heating food inside the jar causes the food to expand and force air out of the jar, creating negative pressure inside the jar. When the food cools, a partial vacuum forms and holds the lid tightly in place, creating an air-tight seal. The more air that is forced out of the jar, the tighter the seal.

venting: *See* exhausting.

water-bath canner: A large stainless or enamel-coated cooking vessel with a rack to hold filled canning jars. It must be deep enough to completely cover jars with one to two inches of water and a few inches of airspace. Boiling water-bath canners are suitable for canning high-acid foods such as fruits, jams, tomatoes, and pickled products.

weighted-gauge pressure canner: One of two types of pressure canners, it is fitted with either a three- or a one-piece weight unit, both with 5-, 10- and 15-pound pressure adjustments. The weight sits on top of the steam vent causing pressure to build up inside the canner. As steam is exhausted through the vent, it causes the weight(s) to rock, indicating that the pressure level has been achieved or is being maintained.

wet-pack: To pack with a liquid when freezing. Includes packing with sugar.

yeast: A microscopic fungi grown from spores that cause fermentation in food.

RESOURCES

The following pages offer a wealth of handy resources related to food preservation.

BURPEE SEEDS

www.burpee.com

Looking to grow your own food to preserve? This site goes beyond just offering seeds and gardening supplies—it also provides great gardening tips and advice.

CANNING ACROSS AMERICA

www.canningacrossamerica.com

This is a collective of cooks, gardeners, and food lovers committed to the revival of canning. Check the site for recipes, resources, and canning events, both local and national. This site provides great support for the novice preserver.

CANNING PANTRY

www.canningpantry.com

This is an online retailer specializing in canning supplies that also provides recipes and instructions.

COOPERATIVE EXTENSION SERVICE

http://lancaster.unl.edu/office/locate.shtml

Your local Cooperative Extension Service is part of a nationwide network dedicated to educating people on issues surrounding agriculture, food safety, and sustainable living, and more. They are your local experts on safe home food preservation. This link will help you to locate an extension service in your state, or you can simply do an Internet search on "Cooperative Extension Service + [your zip code]."

FRESH PRESERVING

www.freshpreserving.com

From the mother company of all things canning, Jarden Home Brands, comes this great site that not only sells canning supplies but also provides instructions, video tutorials, and recipes.

KITCHEN GARDENERS INTERNATIONAL

www.kitchengardeners.org

If you are passionate about sustainable living, this is the site for you. KGI is a nonprofit community dedicated to healthier eating by growing delicious and sustainable food. On their site you'll find great information on home gardening, recipes, local interest groups, and more.

KITCHEN KRAFTS

www.kitchenkrafts.com

Whether you're canning or baking cupcakes, this site has what you need to get it done.

PICK YOUR OWN

www.pickyourown.org/allaboutcanning.htm

If you're looking for a local place to pick your own fruits and veggies, this site offers information nationwide and is updated pretty frequently. Beyond its name, Pick Your Own has information and recipes for canning and freezing.

PLEASANT HILL GRAIN

www.pleasanthillgrain.com

This site offers competitive prices on kitchen gadgets and appliances.

SLOW FOOD USA

www.slowfoodusa.org

Slow Food is a world-wide organization that supports good, clean, and fair food. From the Slow Food USA site, you can learn of programs, events, and local chapters that help to link the pleasure of food with a commitment to community and the environment.

TATTLER REUSABLE CANNING LIDS

www.reusablecanninglids.com

This manufacturer offers reusable, dishwasher-safe, BPA-free plastic lids and rubber bands that can be used with metal screw bands.

UNITED STATES DEPARTMENT OF AGRICULTURE

http://fnic.nal.usda.gov/nal_display/index.php?info_center=4&tax_level=1&tax_subject=242

The USDA maintains a comprehensive site with extensive information about food, diet, nutrition, food safety and more.

USDA NATIONAL CENTER FOR HOME FOOD PRESERVATION

www.uga.edu/nchfp

The USDA includes the National Center for Home Food Preservation, which is the authoritative reference for food preservation and safety. This site provides detailed instructions for and a free, self-paced, online course on home food preservation.

WELLS CANNING COMPANY LIMITED

www.wellscan.ca

Here, you can order canning supplies and appliances such as jars, lids, and pressure canners.

Bibliography

Andress, Elizabeth L. PhD and Judy A. Harrison, PhD. The University of Georgia Cooperative Extension Service. *So Easy to Preserve*, Fifth Ed., The University of Georgia Press, 2006.

Ball Blue Book. Hearthmark, LLC, dba Jarden Home Brands, Daleville, IN, 1909, 2009.

Bubel, Mike and Nancy. *Root Cellaring, Natural Cold Storage of Fruits & Vegetables*. Storey Publishing, 1991, 1979.

Coleman, Eliot. Four-Season Harvest. Chelsea Green Publishing Company, 1992, 1999.

Ekarius, Carol. *Hobby Farm: Living Your Rural Dream for Pleasure and Profit*. BowTie Press, 2005.

Emery, Carla. *Old Fashioned Recipe Book, An Encyclopedia of Country Living*. Bantam Publishing, 1971, 1972, 1973, 1974, 1975, 1977.

The Gardeners & Farmers of Terre Vivante. *Preserving Food without Freezing or Canning*. Chelsea Green Publishing Company, 1999.

Greene, Janet, Hertzberg, Ruth, Vaughan, Beatrice. *Putting Food By*. Penguin Group, 1973, 1975, 1982, 1988.

Ed. Kingry, Judi and Devine, Lauren. *Ball Complete Book of Home Preserving*. Robert Rose, Inc., 2006.

Pollan, Michael. *The Omnivore's Dilemma: A Natural History of Four Meals*. The Penguin Press, 2006.

Schlosser, Eric. *Fast Food Nation: The Dark Side of the All-American Meal*. Houghton Mifflin Company, 2001.

Slagle, Nanci and Santee, Carol. *Big Book of Freezer Cooking*. 30 Day Gourmet Press, 2010.

US Department of Agriculture. Complete Guide to Home Canning and Preserving. BN Publishing, 2008.

Ed. Weber, Karl. *Food Inc.*, Published in the U.S. by PublicAffairs, a member of the Perseus Books Group, 2009

Websites Consulted

Carnegie Mellon Engineering

http://www.cit.cmu.edu/media/press/2008/pr_08_apr18a.html

Clemson Cooperative Extension Service

Food Safety Issues: http://www.clemson.edu/extension/hgic/food/food_safety/preservation/

Favorite Freezer Food

http://www.favoritefreezerfoods.com/freezer-containers.html

Health Library

http://healthlibrary.epnet.com/GetContent.aspx?token=a4c1f00b-d245-44f2-a90e-20b047f84 a6a&chunkiid=160561

Hobby Farm Home

http://www.hobbyfarms.com/food-and-kitchen/canning-fruits-vegetables-how-to-preserve. aspx

Jarden Corporation:

http://jarden.com/

Pick Your Own

http://www.pickyourown.org/allaboutcanning.htm

University of California, Davis

http://fruitvegquality.ucdavis.edu/publications/MaxFoodVegApril%202006.pdf

National Center for Home Food Preservation

http://www.uga.edu/nchfp/

USDA Food Safety and Inspection Service—Specific Preservation Issues: Freezing

http://www.fsis.usda.gov/Fact_Sheets/Focus_On_Freezing/index.asp

INDEX

PHOTO CREDITS

Illustrations by Tom Kimball
/SS = Shutterstock.com
/Flickr = from Flickr under
the Creative Commons License

page 1: Lilyana Vynogradova/SS
page 4: Amie Fedora/Flickr
page 6: Psrobin/Flickr
page 7: Maya83/Flickr
page 9: Charles Amundson/SS
page 10: Julie DeGuia/SS
page 11: psrobin/Flickr
page 12 : *(top)* Subbotina Anna/SS,
(bottom) Inta Eihmane/SS
page 13: Stevie Rocco/Flickr
page 14 : *(top)* Elena Elisseeva/SS,
(bottom) Alexander Paterov/SS
page 15: Alexander Ryabintsev/SS
page 16: igor kisselev/SS
page 17: Charles Amundson/SS
page 19: Amie Fedora/Flickr
page 20: Stew Hardie/SS
page 21: BestPhoto1/SS
page 22: SunnyS/SS
page 23: Liv friis-larsen/SS
page 24 : *(top)* Sandra Cunningham/SS,
(bottom) Kenneth V. Pilon/SS
page 25: Ambient Ideas/SS
page 26: Torsten Schon/SS
page 30: Jean Fogle
page 31: Baloncici/SS
page 32: Josef Mohyla/SS
page 33: TDMuldoon/SS
page 35: Pinkcandy/SS
page 36: Silvia Bogdanski/SS
page 38: ilovebutter/Flickr
page 40: yamix/SS
page 42: Fotokostic/SS
page 44: courtesy of Rubbermaid/Flickr
page 48: Jean Fogle
page 49: Tomislav Pinter/SS
page 50: Falkiewicz Henryk/SS

page 51: Liv friis-larsen/SS
page 52: RomanSo/SS
page 53: Wiktory/SS
page 54 : *(top)* Pinkcandy/SS,
(bottom) AdamEdwards/SS
page 55: Josh Resnick/SS
page 57: whitneyinchicago/Flickr
page 58: Cogipix/SS
page 59: Marie C Fields/SS
page 60: anna_bobrowska/SS
page 61: Jean Fogle
page 62: David P. Smith/SS
page 63: matka_Wariatka/SS
page 64: theblack/SS
page 66: Luiz Rocha/SS
page 67: Wiktory/SS
page 69: Lilyana Vynogradova/SS
page 70: Rachel Tayse/Flickr
page 71: sarsmis/SS
page 72: Jean Fogle
page 77: Amie Fedora/Flickr
page 78: Graham Taylor Photography/SS
page 79 : *(top)* Jean Fogle,
(bottom) Carissa Rogers/Flickr
page 80 : *(top)* Southern Foodways Alliance/Flickr,
(bottom) Elenadan/Flickr
page 82 : CarissaRogers/Flickr
page 83 : *(top)* daisybush/Flickr,
(bottom) MegaHammond/Flickr
page 84 : *(both)* Jean Fogle
page 86 : *(top)* Carissa Rogers/Flickr,
(bottom) psrobin/Flickr
page 88: Jean Fogle
page 89 : *(top)* Christina Richards/SS,
(bottom) Tim Wilson/Flickr
page 90: Marie C Fields/SS
page 91: matka_Wariatka/SS
page 92: Lilyana Vynogradova/SS
page 93: Marie C Fields/SS
page 94 : *(top)* ElenaGaak/SS,
(bottom) Mike Willis/Flickr
page 95: Olga Utlyakova/SS
page 96: Will Merydith/Flickr

page 97: BlueberryFiles/Flickr

page 98: Jean Fogle

page 99: avs/SS

pages 100–102: Jean Fogle

page 104: ElenaGaak/SS

page 105: Teresa Kasprzycka/SS

page 106: Jean Fogle

page 108: Charlotte Lake/SS

page 109: TheBittenWord.com

page 110: Tamy Nichole Thomason/SS

page 111: mariko/Flickr

page 112: margouillat photo/SS

page 115: sarsmis/SS

page 117: IngridHS/SS

page 118: Fotogiunta/SS

page 120: Jean Fogle

page 121: Burning Light Photography/SS

page 122: BestPhoto1/SS

page 122: Karen Sarraga/SS

page 123: Tomo Jesenicnik/SS

page 124 : (top) Valentyn Volkov/SS, (bottom) Subbotina Anna/SS

page 125: Sandra Cunningham/SS

page 126: Leon Chong/SS

page 128 : (top) IngridHS/SS, (bottom) Amie Fedora/Flickr

page 130 : (top) .christie./Flickr, (bottom) stockstudios/SS

page 131: Lilyana Vynogradova/SS

page 132: (all) IngridHS/SS

page 133: Chris leachman/SS

page 134 : (top) Massimiliano Pieraccini/SS, (bottom) Jean Fogle

page 135: Viktor1/SS

page 136: picamaniac/SS

page 137 : (top) kukuruxa/SS, (bottom) Jiri Hera/SS

page 139: Jean Fogle

page 140: tlorna/SS

page 141: Heike Rau/SS

page 142: jamieanne/Flickr

page 143: Wiktory/SS

page 144: Digivic/SS

page 145: jeffreyw/Flickr

page 148: eren | thisvintagechica/Flickr

page 149 : (top) Amie Fedora/Flickr, (middle) Jean Fogle, (bottom) Amie Fedora/Flickr

page 150 : (both) Amie Fedora/Flickr

page 153 : (top) Jim Champion/Flickr, (bottom) Bratwustle/SS

page 155: David P. Smith/SS

page 156 : (top) Andrea Skjold/SS, (bottom) Viktor1/SS

page 157: Studiotouch/SS

page 158 : (top) sarsmis/SS, (bottom) Gordon Swanson/SS

page 159 : (top) Dan Cavallari/SS, (bottom) Fotoksa/SS

page 160 : (both) Chris Martin/Flickr

page 161: Chris Martin/Flickr

page 162: Chris Martin/Flickr

page 163: Jean Fogle

page 164: Elena Ray/SS

page 167: (top) Stephanie Frey/SS, (middle) Jean Fogle, (bottom right) Jean Fogle, (bottom left) Lori_NY/Flickr

page 168: Jean Fogle

page 169: Josh Resnick/SS

page 170: Jill Battaglia/SS

page 172: jordache/SS

page 174: whitneyinchicago/Flickr

page 175: Josh Resnick/SS

page 176: (top and middle) Chris Martin/Flickr, (bottom) Ben Husmann/Flickr

page 177: Catherine Murray/SS

page 178: Bochkarev Photography/SS

page 179 : (both) Lenore Edman/Flickr

page 180: svry/SS

page 181: Olga Miltsova/SS

page 182: hd connelly/SS

page 185: Raw.lik.2/SS

page 186 : (top) Kim Knoch/Flickr, (bottom) marekuliasz/SS

page 189: Maya83/Flickr

page 191: Amie Fedora/Flickr

page 195: Jean Fogle/Flickr

page 207: Robyn Mackenzie/SS

About the Author

Jackie Callahan Parente is a freelance writer living in a suburb outside Hartford, Connecticut. She's worked with words as writer, editor, tech writer, and food writer for more years than she'd care to admit. Food writing blends her love of words with her passion and pleasure in gardening, cooking, home food preservation, and eating locally and sustainably. A member of Slow Food USA and Canning Across America, she brings to Can It! experience garnered over several decades of preserving food at home. In addition to this book, she authors a popular food blog (Raspberries, Rabbits, and Rutabagas), and offers classes in home food preservation. Jackie has owned her own freelance writing company— Editorial Services, LLC—since 1996. Check her out at either www.editorial-services.com or http://raspberriesrabbitsrutabagas.com.